Handmade Paper
from
Naturals

Handmade Paper from Naturals

Diane Flowers

LARK BOOKS

A Division of Sterling Publishing Co., Inc.

New York / London

Prolific Impressions Production Staff:

Editor in Chief: Mickey Baskett
Copy Editor: Phyllis Mueller
Graphics: Karen Turpin
Styling: Lenos Key
Photography: Jerry Mucklow, Joel Tressler
Administration: Jim Baskett
Indexing: Miche Baskett

Library of Congress Cataloging-in-Publication Data

Flowers, Diane D., 1952-
  Handmade paper from naturals / Diane Flowers.
      p. cm.
  Includes index.
  ISBN 978-1-60059-447-2 (hbk. : alk. paper)
  1. Papermaking. 2. Fiber plants. 3. Paper, Handmade. I. Title.
  TS1124.5.F56 2008
  676'.22--dc22

                        2008038342

10 9 8 7 6 5 4 3 2 1

First Edition

Published by Lark Books, A Division of
Sterling Publishing Co., Inc.
387 Park Avenue South, New York, NY 10016

© 2009, Prolific Impressions, Inc.

Distributed in Canada by Sterling Publishing,
c/o Canadian Manda Group, 165 Dufferin Street
Toronto, Ontario, Canada M6K 3H6

Distributed in the United Kingdom by GMC Distribution Services,
Castle Place, 166 High Street, Lewes, East Sussex, England BN7 1XU

Distributed in Australia by Capricorn Link (Australia) Pty Ltd.,
P.O. Box 704, Windsor, NSW 2756 Australia

If you have questions or comments about this book, please contact:
Lark Books, 67 Broadway, Asheville, NC 28801; (828) 253-0467

Manufactured in China

ISBN-13: 978-1-60059-447-2

For information about custom editions, special sales, premium and corporate purchases, please contact Sterling Special Sales Department at 800-805-5489 or specialsales@sterlingpub.com.

ABOUT THE AUTHOR
Diane Flowers

Diane Flowers is a self-taught creative designer and well known craft book author. She enjoys working with natural plant materials and all varieties of artificial flowers to create her unique designs. Diane started out designing, assembling, and selling her own lines of home decorating accessories; today, she sells her designs to manufacturers and magazine and book editors. She is the author of *Silk Flowers for Every Season* (North Light, 2005) and *Preserved Flowers, Pressed and Dried* (Sterling, 2006).

You can contact Diane and see more of her work on her company website, www.MFTEnterprises.com.

THANKS

• Many thanks to my husband, Ed, for contributing his favorite pair of worn-out blue jeans and for his continued support, which allows me to pursue my passion for designing.

• An extra big thank you to my talented daughter-in-law designer, JoyAnn, and her husband, my son Kenon, who both so willingly jumped in to help me when I most needed it. You can see more of her work at www.joyajewelry.etsy.com.

• And one last very special thank you to Mickey Baskett, the editor and producer of my last book, and also this one. Mickey has a wonderful talent for very graciously providing her professional support and expertise in creating very informative and fabulous books.

Acknowledgements

My personal thanks go to the following people and companies who so generously provided their products to support the completion of this book: **Kim Grummer and Arnold Grummer's Inc.** for supporting my efforts by providing so many of their wonderful products, including kits, pulps, additives, molds, and deckles. Many thanks to **Sharon Currier and Dow Chemical Co.** for Styrofoam™ brand foam products; to **Krylon** for Preserve It, spray sealers, antiquing spray, and Make It Acid Free spray; to **Tombow** for glue; to **Nature's Pressed** for pressed flowers and leaves; and to **Mary and Conjoined Creations, Inc.** (www.confoinedcreations.com) for the beautiful colors of natural soy fibers; and also the Yahoo papermaking group for inspiration.

CONTENTS

CHAPTER 1.

CHAPTER 2.

CHAPTER 3.

PAGE 98

PAGE 111

PAGE 123

Handmade Paper: Fun *and* Easy

CREATING YOUR OWN HANDMADE PAPER WITH NATURAL PLANT MATERIALS IS FUN, AND IT'S MUCH EASIER THAN YOU MIGHT THINK. Plus there is so much opportunity to use your creativity to make unique and beautiful papers. Start by pulverizing some junk mail, add in some natural plant materials, form it on a mesh mold—and the result is a truly beautiful and unique sheet of handmade paper.

The first step in paper-making is making paper pulp. You can make your own pulp by blending recycled papers with water.

Paper is made of interlocking fibers held together by cellulose, a natural plant material. Paper sheets are formed using a frame mold with a screen mesh bottom, some water, and paper pulp. The mold is placed in a vat of water and the pulp is added. As the mold is lifted out of the water a layer of interlocking fibers remains on the surface of the screen. Water, which helps the fibers to expand and bond together, is drained through the bottom of the mold. More water must be removed before the paper sheet is pressed and dried.

To make paper you need pulp, which is made of some type of cellulosic material, such as wood pulp or cotton fibers or previously made paper. The easiest way to make your own paper pulp is to recycle junk mail or any paper that you might otherwise throw away. All kinds of plant material, including grasses, vegetables, flowers, leaves, seeds, and needles, can be added to paper with beautiful results. Although commercial paper makers use large machines to beat their pulps, for making small amounts of paper an everyday food blender works just fine.

A Brief History of Paper Making

We all handle paper every day. Paper is the medium for many types of written communications, from letters and bills to advertising circulars to to-do lists and receipts and birthday cards. But this wasn't always the case. Many different substances were used as writing surfaces before paper was developed. The Chinese inscribed marks on bones. The Babylonians carved characters on clay bricks and tablets. Others recorded information on metals, pieces of wood, leaves, and tree bark. Parchment made from the skins of sheep and goats was used in Europe probably as early as 1500 B.C.E., and vellum was made from the unsplit skins of young calves, goats, and lambs. In Egypt, hieroglyphs were carved in monuments of stone and written on papyrus. Although the papyrus plant can be beaten and made into paper, traditional papyrus was made by cutting strips of the plant's stalk into lengths, overlapping them side by side, and pounding them flat. Technically speaking, it wasn't paper; the actual plant materials used depended on what was locally available, and varied from place to place.

Ts'ai Lun, an emperor's eunuch in China, is credited with the invention of paper in 105 C.E., though the exact year is in dispute. Some historians maintain paper was invented several centuries earlier, and that Ts'ai Lun most likely refined the process. By 615 the paper making had spread to Japan, arriving in the Arab regions sometime around 750, and reaching Egypt and Morocco in the 10th century. Paper making came to Europe around 1151, and the first paper mill began production around 1488. Paper making was first introduced in the United States by William Rittenhouse in 1690 in Germantown, Pennsylvania. The first paper making machine was invented in France by Nicholas Louis Robert in 1798 and perfected in England in the early 1800s by the Fourdrinier brothers.

Dard Hunter, who lived and worked in the early 1900s at his studio on his inherited estate, Mountain House, in Chillicothe, Ohio, is considered the father of the modern hand paper-making revival. Hunter documented his findings in his book *The History and Technique of an Ancient Craft*. Many others have researched the history of making paper, but no single book is nearly as complete as Hunter's. His collections and archives are currently located at the Robert C. Williams American Museum of Papermaking in Atlanta, Georgia.

Hand paper making enjoyed a second revival during the 1960s and 70s as artists developed paper pulp sculptures and custom prints for clients. The revival continues today with many colleges and universities offering classes, apprenticeships, and internships to pass on the knowledge of paper making and preserve the tradition for future generations.

Getting Started

This book is intended for beginner papermakers. It includes the step-by-step instructions for the basic paper making process and tells how to get started making papers with natural materials that are easy to find. It also includes recipes for more than 25 types of handmade papers and two dozen projects for creating unique gifts and decorative items with your handmade papers that you will be proud to display in your home and share with your friends and family.

Like any new endeavor, paper making may require a little practice and experimentation. If your first attempts are not successful, don't despair—just keep trying. You'll discover what works for you. Feel free to use the recipes and projects in this book to develop your own paper making style.

1.

PAPER MAKING SUPPLIES

This chapter explains and pictures the basic supplies and tools you will need to be successful at papermaking. Some items you will be able to find around your house. Other items you will find at craft or hobby stores as well as online sources. Several paper making suppliers offer kits that contain everything you need to make paper as well as additives and other materials.

▶ Be safe!

After using household tools for making paper, they should **never** be used for preparing or storing food. Keep them with your craft supplies. It is a good idea to label spoons, bowls, or other household items with a note that says "Use for Paper Making only."

PAPER PULP

Paper pulp is the fiber source for making paper. You can make this from paper you have or you can buy pulp that is already processed and ready to use. Below are some guidelines for choosing paper pulp.

Prepared Paper Pulp

High quality prepared fibers and pulps can be purchased from art supply stores and paper making suppliers, which usually include instructions for preparing and using them. Cotton and abaca are the most common prepared fibers. Both fibers are processed in the blender in the same way that recycled paper is processed.

Cotton linter makes an opaque, soft sheet. It is made from the seed hair fiber that is a result of the cotton ginning process. Cotton may come in sheets that are easily torn or in bags of loose pulp pieces that do not require tearing.

Abaca is made from the leaf stalks of banana plants. Abaca is very thick and hard to tear. It should be soaked in water before adding to your blender.

Paper pulps

Papers for making recycled pulp

Recycled Paper to Use for Pulp

Pulp can also be made by recycling junk mail or any other kinds of papers you have. Sources of recycled pulp include shredded office papers, advertising circulars, postcards, greeting cards, unused credit card applications, envelopes, shipping and packing paper, wrapping paper, tissue paper, pages from books and magazines, brown paper bags, and unused napkins or paper plates. Newspaper, though readily available, will not make a strong thick paper and is not a good choice for pulp making.

The quality of your sheets will only be as good as the quality of the recycled paper you use. One way to judge paper's quality is by its source. Banks, cultural organizations, and image-conscious entities use higher quality paper. (Think symphony programs or stationery from an elected official.) Lower quality paper, such as magazine pages, will produce nice gray sheets, but the ink may form a film that will coat your mold, screen, and couching sheets. It's best to opt for quality papers when you recycle.

Business communication papers and envelopes, custom bags from upscale retailers, wrapping papers, plain brown bags, and tissue papers are good sources for color.

The color of the recycled paper you use will affect the resulting color of your handmade paper. However, there is no good way to predict what the resulting color might be except through experimentation. Since most colored construction papers bleed when wet, I only use them when I want that appearance in my sheets.

MOLDS

Molds are used to make individual sheets of paper. They are frames with wire screen attached to the bottom. You can make your own molds or purchase them from specialty paper making suppliers.

The two basic types of molds are dip molds and pour molds. With a **pour mold**, the paper pulp is poured into the mold after the mold is placed in a vat of water. The mold is raised up through the water, and the pulp stays on the screen at the bottom of the mold. With a **dip mold**, the mold is dipped into a vat of water to which paper pulp has been added. The sides of a pour mold are taller than those of the dip mold. With practice, you can use a pour mold for dipping, but the dip mold's shorter sides make the process a little easier.

BLENDER

Most household food blenders work perfectly for blending water with paper pulp. One with multiple speeds and a pulse button is handy when using fragile flowers and botanicals. Choose a blender with a larger container—one that will allow the addition of at least three cups of water to the dry paper pulp. CAUTION! Once you've used a blender for paper making, **never** use it again for food preparation.

▶ HOW TO MAKE YOUR OWN MOLD

It is easy to make your own dip mold. Use waterproof staples or screws to attach rustproof screen to a wood frame or embroidery hoop. Support the screen from the bottom with ¼" mesh hardware cloth. To avoid cutting your hands, cover the edges of the wire with duct tape. For added protection from water damage, paint the wooden frame pieces with several coats of water-resistant polyurethane.

With use, the wire screen and mesh in homemade molds will eventually sag and need to be replaced. To prolong the life of your screen, attach a piece of plastic grid (the kind used in fluorescent light fixtures) to the frame under the screening to provide extra support.

Paper making suppliers offer a polypropylene screen that can be used instead of wire screening that lasts longer than other screening materials. It is glued to the frame, and then made taut by heating with a hair dryer.

Pictured on the opposite page, left to right: Pour mold, handmade dip mold, purchased dip mold

OTHER MOLDING SUPPLIES

Deckles

Deckles are forms that look like cut out stencils that are placed inside the mold to make special sizes and shapes of papers. They are made of sturdy plastic or other waterproof materials. You can buy deckles or make your own using ¼" thick plastic sheets or plastic foam. An envelope deckle is easy to make: Take apart an envelope of the desired size, trace around it on a piece of plastic or plastic foam, and cut out the traced shape, leaving the outline.

Vat

The vat is a large plastic tub. It should be deep enough to hold at least 3" of water and your mold. To determine the size you need, measure your mold and add 6" to the outside dimensions. For example, if your mold is 9" x 12", you'll want a vat that measures at least 15" x 18".

Whisk

Use a whisk to mix the pulp after pouring the pulp into a mold or vat. A whisk can also be used to mix and position materials inside the mold or vat.

Additives

Available in liquid or powder form, acid free additives can be added to wet pulp before blending to ensure smooth, acid free sheets of paper. Buy them from paper making suppliers, and follow the package instructions for use.

Measuring Cups & Spoons

Glass and plastic measuring cups are indispensable for measuring water, paper pulp, and plant materials. Measuring spoons are needed for measuring additives.

Strainers & Netting Fabric

Strainers are used for straining pulp after blending. A strainer lined with netting fabric is useful for quickly removing water from wet pulp to prepare the pulp for storage. Strainers are also used to remove pulp from a tub or vat when the pulp-and-water (slurry) mixture is too thick.

▶ TIP – Use pH test strips to determine the level of acidity in paper pulp when you want to make archival-quality papers. Anything less than 8.5 is considered acid free.

Pictured on opposite page:
1 – Deckles
2 – Vat
3 – Whisk
4 – pH strips
5 – Acid free additive
6 – Glass measuring cups
7 – Plastic measuring cups
8 – Strainers
9 – Measuring spoons

SUPPLIES FOR DRYING PAPER

After the sheets are molded and pulled from the water vat, they then have to be couched and dried. Couching (rhymes with "pooching") is the process of removing water from wet paper sheets after they are removed from the mold. After the sheets have been couched they are then left to dry thoroughly. There are several options you can choose for the final drying of your handmade paper sheets.

Couch Sheets

Couch sheets are highly absorbent sheets made to soak up water from the wet paper. Couch sheets should be rinsed after each use. After they are dry (this can take several hours), they can be reused. Buy them from paper making suppliers. Other types of cloth materials can be used for couching, such as felt, blankets, blotter paper, or mesh dishcloths. Mesh dishcloths are not as absorbent or efficient as the other materials.

Waterproof Tray (or Couching Tray)

Use this tray to hold the wet paper sheet and couch sheets while removing (couching) water from the paper. This has to be perfectly flat, hard, and smooth. You could put a plastic cutting board inside a plastic lid from a tub to create a hard, smooth waterproof tray.

Heatproof Board

You will need this during the drying and pressing stage when using an iron for the drying process.

Mesh Dishcloths

Reusable, disposable mesh cleaning cloths or dishcloths, which are available at supermarkets, can be used to absorb water and protect paper sheets during the pressing and drying stage when using an iron. They are large enough to cover both sides of an 8½" x 11" sheet of paper, dry quickly, and can be ironed dry for quick reuse.

Sponges

Regular household sponges are used to remove (couch) water from wet paper sheets.

Pressing Block & Roller Tool

These tools help press water from the paper sheets during couching. A pressing block is a small piece of solid, flat wood; a roller tool can be made of hard rubber, plastic, or wood.

Paper Presses—Drying Option 1

A **homemade paper press** can be made by layering wet paper sheets between several dry couch sheets and placing them between two pieces of polyurethane-coated wood. C-clamps are used to hold and press the paper and wood.

Paper press that you can purchase for professional results.

Pictured opposite page:
1 – Couch sheet
2 – Lid from a plastic tub used for couching tray
3 – Plastic heatproof board
4 – Pressing block
5 – Roller tool
6 – Wire racks
7 – Sponges
8 – Mesh dishcloth
9 – Protective sprays

▶ **TIP – PROTECTIVE SPRAYS**

Fixatives, spray sealers, and acid free sprays can be used to protect dry papers from the elements. Always use sprays outdoors and allow the sprayed papers and other materials to dry completely before handling them. Spraying dried plants and flowers with a sealer before mixing them with wet pulp helps them retain color and avoid bleeding.

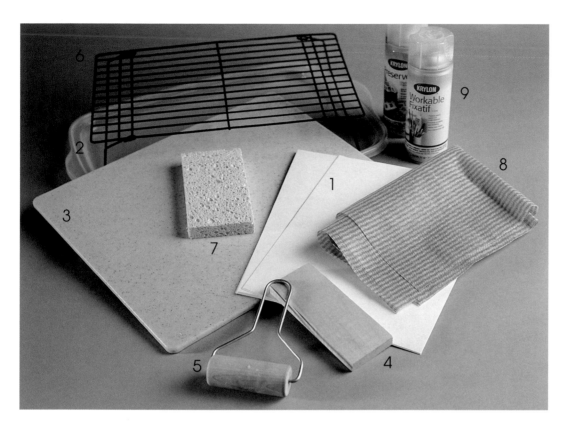

As an option, **professional paper presses** can be purchased. They create beautiful, flat, even sheets of paper. The pressure they provide helps compress the fibers, forming a denser and stronger bond that makes a higher quality, more durable sheet of paper.

Drying Racks–Drying Option 2

Stackable wire racks that allow air to circulate around the wet sheets of paper can be used for air drying. Air drying produces a more textured paper that does not dry completely flat. The papers will curl naturally but will flatten if glued to a flat surface.

Drying Box–Drying Option 3

To speed the drying process when making several sheets of paper, you can make a drying box using a box fan, pieces of cardboard, and couch sheets or paper blotter drying sheets. For best results use bi-wall or tri-wall cardboard (two or three pieces laminated together) for making your drying box.
Here's how:
1. Cut pieces of cardboard slightly larger than your paper sheets. Position the corrugated channels running the same direction on all the pieces. You can stack the pieces as tall as your box fan.

2. Place the damp paper sheets between drying sheets and stack them between the cardboard pieces. Place the stack in front of the fan, aligning the channels in the cardboard pieces so the air can flow through them. Position two pieces of cardboard against the sides of the stack.
3. Secure the side pieces and the top with weights, blocks, or bricks so the stacked papers and cardboard pieces will not move when the fan blows air through them.
4. Turn the fan on high speed. The sheets should be dry in 24 hours.

Microwave–Drying Option 4

Your microwave oven can be used to speed the paper pressing and drying processes. A purchased microwave flower press can be used for drying small sheets of paper, or you can make a microwave paper press by layering paper towels between two pieces of cardboard and securing them with rubber bands.

Iron–Drying Option 5

When you are in a hurry to dry your paper sheets, use a medium to hot iron to speed drying after couching. Always place a dry mesh dishcloth or any other thin cloth between the iron and the paper sheet; when the cloth gets wet, swap it for a dry one. An iron with a non-stick soleplate works best.

PLANT PREPARATION SUPPLIES

In the *Paper Making Recipes* section, you'll find instructions for preparing and using different types of plant materials, including fresh leaves and flowers, dried flowers and herbs, coffee, tea, spices, seeds, and fibers. Some plant materials require cooking in an alkaline solution to break down the fibers before blending them with paper pulp or using them to make paper; others require boiling, soaking, or chopping. Some only need to be torn into small pieces.

Pots & Utensils

Cook plants you're preparing for paper making in non-reactive pots—ones that are made of stainless steel or glass or are enamel-coated. Use stainless steel or enamel-coated utensils or wooden spoons for stirring. **Never** use pots and utensils that you've used for paper making for cooking food. **Always** cook plant materials outside on a hot plate or outdoor stovetop.

Alkalizing Agents

Soda ash, washing soda, and fireplace ashes can be added to water to make an alkaline cooking solution for plant materials. Soda ash can be purchased from paper making suppliers; washing soda can be found at most grocery stores. Some papermakers claim they achieve the same results with washing soda and soda ash; others maintain washing soda leaves a residue in the paper, while soda ash does not. Use extreme care—alkaline compounds can be caustic. Wear protective clothing, eye protection, and gloves. Avoid splashing yourself and work outdoors. *For instructions for using alkalizing agents, see "Preparing Plant Materials" in the* Paper Making Recipes *section.*

Measuring Cups & Spoons

You'll need glass and plastic measuring cups and plastic measuring spoons to measure amounts of water, alkalizing solutions, plant materials, and additives.

Strainer & Netting Fabric

Use a strainer for draining, rinsing, and separating plant material from water after cooking. Line the strainer with netting fabric when straining small pieces of boiled plant material.

MAKING YOUR OWN FIREPLACE ASH SOLUTION

Follow these steps to make an alkaline solution using wood ashes from your fireplace or wood stove. Be Safe! Work outdoors and wear protective gear to protect yourself from accidental splashes.

1. Fill a large stainless steel, enamel-coated, or glass pot halfway with ashes. Add cold water to the pot until it is three-quarters full.
2. Stir the ashes and water while bringing to a boil. Let boil 30 minutes.
3. Remove from heat. Allow the mixture to settle overnight.
4. Strain and save the alkaline solution. Discard the wet ashes.

Pictured on opposite page:
1 – Cooking pot
2 – Wooden spoon
3 – Hot plate
4 – Strainer
5 – Alkalizing agent
6 – Measuring cups
7 – Measuring spoons

CRAFTING SUPPLIES

These are some of the supplies you'll need for creating some of the special papers and the handmade paper projects in this book. The recipes in the *Paper Making Recipes* section and the individual project instructions in the Handmade Paper Projects section tell you how and when these supplies are used.

Mechanical Presses

Flower pressing kits that contain everything you need to press flowers and leaves can be purchased, or you can make your own with two pieces of wood, some papers, cardboard, and four bolts and wing nuts.

Microwave Presses

A flower press specifically made for use in the microwave is an easy way to press flowers and leaves quickly. Special microwave presses can be purchased or a homemade microwave flower press can be made with two pieces of cardboard, paper towels, and rubber bands.

Iron & Wax Paper

Still another option for pressing flowers and leaves is to use a hot dry iron and wax paper. Simply position the leaves or flowers between two pieces of wax paper and slowly move the iron across them. Lift the wax paper and allow the leaves and flowers to cool before handling them.

Pieces of wax paper are also used to separate and protect newly glued book covers and pages before placing them in a press to dry.

Tweezers

Use tweezers to handle fragile dried and pressed plant materials and flowers.

Adhesives

Most types of basic crafting glues that dry clear will work well with dried and pressed plant materials, flowers, and leaves when adding them to dried sheets of handmade papers. You may also want to try these specialty glues for your paper making projects:

- PVA (polyvinyl acetate) is a glue used by many papermakers and bookmakers. It is strong, dries clear, and contains a preservative that protects papers and dried materials from mold.
- Methyl cellulose, an archival waterbased adhesive, can be easily removed with water. Buy it from papermaking suppliers.
- Use decoupage gel to attach decorative elements to your papers and to seal and protect them.
- For making envelopes, there's a special glue you can put on the flap that is activated when moistened.

▶ **TIP** – Another option for pressing and drying flowers and leaves is to use your old telephone directories and some weights. The pages of the directory are absorbent and make great drying sheets. Simply place the plants between the pages of the phone books, put weights on top, and allow the plants to dry undisturbed.

▶ **TIP** – One of my favorite tools for tearing paper is a metal deckle edge ruler—I use it for making a straight deckle edge on stationery, envelopes, and cards.

Pictured on opposite page:
Crafting Supplies
1 – Wax paper
2 – Flower presses
3 – Paper trimmer
4 – Adhesives
5 – Cutting mat
6 – Craft knife
7 – Rotary cutter
8 – Metal ruler
9 – Deckle edge ruler
10 – Tweezers

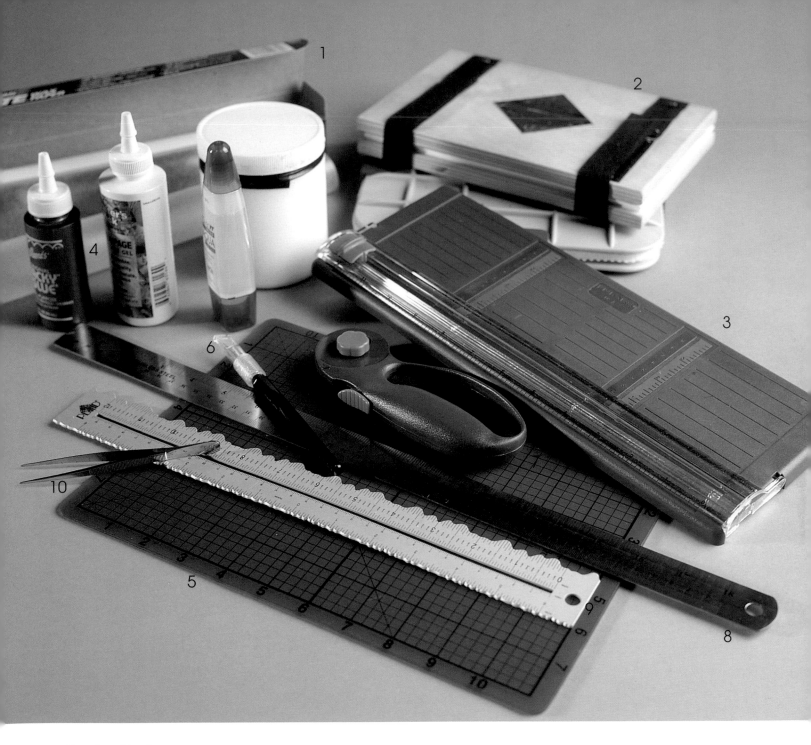

Cutting Tools

Use scissors, a rotary cutter with decorative blades, or a craft knife to cut your papers. A paper trimmer with a sliding blade is useful for card making and trimming larger paper sheets.

Rulers

A clear plastic ruler is useful for lining up different materials when layering papers and for making straight seams or borders while cutting or tearing. You'll want a metal ruler to use as a guide when you're cutting straight lines with a craft knife.

Cutting Mat

A self healing cutting mat will protect your work surface and prolong the life of your blades and cutting tools.

2.

THE PAPER MAKING PROCESS

Now you are ready to set up your work area and start making paper. This section shows you, step by step, how to make handmade paper. Paper making is basically a four-step process: sheet forming, couching, pressing, and drying.

▶ *Keep a Paper Making Diary*

After going through the process of making a sheet of paper, you may discover that a certain sheet of recycled paper or a particular plant or flower you added to your pulp did not produce the result you hoped for. By keeping a diary to record what you did and what materials you used, you can keep track of your successes and learn from past mistakes (and avoid repeating them). The more details you record, the more you will learn as you experiment with different materials and processes. With practice, some techniques will become second nature. Each sheet you make will teach you something new.

PAPER MAKING OVERVIEW

Before you start to make paper, it's a good idea to educate yourself about the process. Setting up your work area properly and understanding the flow of the process will help ensure fabulous results. I recommend that you read this chapter to familiarize yourself with the steps before you start. After you make your first sheet, you can make adjustments and begin to develop your own techniques. Several steps and a lot of water are involved in making a sheet of paper. The basic steps are outlined below. Details appear on the following pages.

1 **Prepare.** Select your pulp materials, plant materials, and additives and prepare them for processing in the blender.

2 **Blend your pulp.** Place your pulp in a blender and add water.

3 **Pour.** Pour the blended pulp into a vat of water (If you're using a dip mold) or into your mold in a vat of water (If you're using a pour mold).

4 **Stir.** Stir the pulp to mix it with the water in the vat so that it floats freely and loosely in the water.

5 **Lift.** Lift the mold out of the water. The sheet of paper will be formed as the water drains away from the pulp that remains on the screen at the bottom of the mold.

6 **Remove from mold.** Remove the wet pulp sheet from the mold and place it on top of a couch sheet on a waterproof tray.

7 **Begin removing water.** Cover the wet pulp sheet with a dry couch sheet. Press a sponge over the couch sheet to remove the excess water.

8 **Remove more water.** Wring the excess water from the sponge. Turn over the wet pulp sheet and the two couch sheets. Remove the top wet couch sheet.

9 **Continue removing water.** Place a dry couch sheet over the wet pulp sheet. Press it with the sponge. Repeat wringing the sponge, turning over the sheets, exchanging the wet couch sheets for dry ones, and pressing them with the sponge until the sponge cannot remove any more water.

10 **Dry.** Press and dry the sheet using a combination of ironing, placing it in a press, and/or microwaving, or simply allow it to air dry.

WORK AREA SET UP

Because so much water is used in making paper, it is worth your time and effort to organize your work area to avoid getting everything wet.

Work outdoors if you can

Working outdoors eliminates the need to worry about cleaning up water that might escape from the vat or tub. Perform all cooking in a well-ventilated area. If using alkaline solutions, always cook outside.

Be safe!

Wear a protective mask and gloves when cooking with alkaline solutions. Protect yourself from accidental splashes and spills and avoid exposure to fumes. Make sure your work area is free of electrical hazards. Keep extension cords away from faucets and hoses.

Work near your water source

Blending is more efficient if you do not have to transport water. Position your vat or tub of water close to your water source.

Choose a comfortable height

Position your vat or tub of water at a comfortable height which allows you to see inside the mold and deckle when they are inside the tub or vat.

Arrange your work table

Place a waterproof tray beside your tub or vat for couching. Allow space on your work table beside your waterproof couching tray for storing your wet mold and deckle. Keep extra couch sheets available beside your couching tray.

RECYCLING WATER

I recycle the water from our dehumidifier for paper making. During the summer I try to reuse the water that drips out of our air conditioner. (Most of the time I only need a bucketful, which can easily be collected in just a few hours.)

But **do not** use recycled water when making archival quality papers. As a precaution, test your water and pulp to be sure they are pH neutral before making archival quality sheets. See "About pH Levels" for more information.

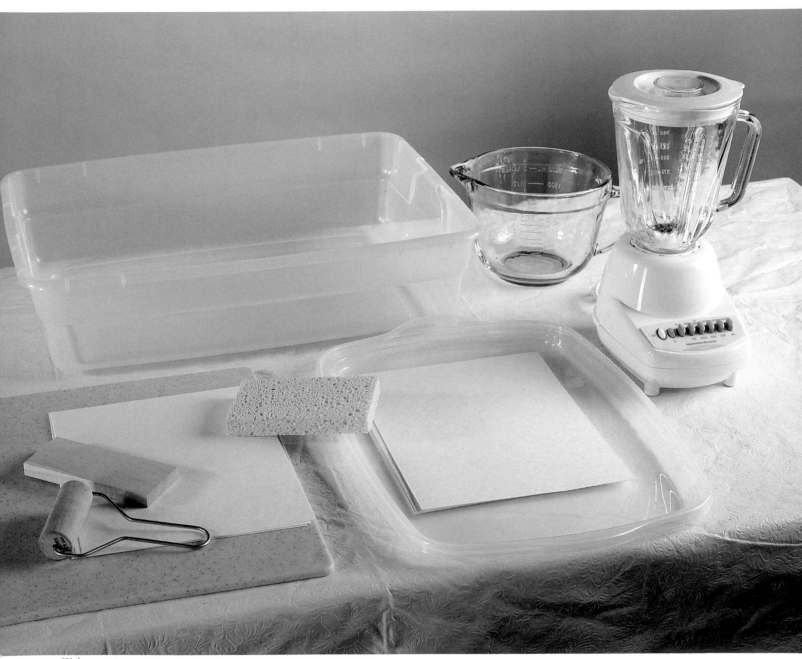

Work space set up

MAKING THE PAPER PULP

There are many different ways to prepare paper pulp. Different processes yield different results—thick or thin papers, smooth or rough, translucent or opaque are only a few of the variations. With experimentation and experience you will learn what works best for you.

These instructions are for making one cup of basic recycled pulp that is used in most of the recipes in this book. Approximately five sheets of recycled 8½" x 11" paper will make three or more cups of wet pulp or one cup of strained dry pulp that can be stored and used later. One cup of strained dry pulp will make one or two sheets of 8½" x 11" paper, depending on the desired thickness.

Photo 1 – Tearing the paper.

Pulverizing the Paper

1. Tear five 8½" x 11" sheets of recycled paper into 2" squares. (Photo 1)
2. Pour water in your blender container until it's about half full. Add the paper pieces to the water in the blender container. Some papermakers prefer to soak the torn paper for one hour or longer before blending. I recommend soaking when using thicker paper or fibers. Normally soaking is not required if using standard thickness papers. (Photo 2)
3. Add more water until the blender container is about three-quarters full. Blend at medium speed for about 30 seconds or until at least half of the fibers are mushy and almost dissolved. (Photo 3, Photo 4)

Photo 2 – Putting the paper pieces in the blender.

Photo 3 – Starting to blend.

4. To determine if the pulp is ready, put a small amount in a jar of cold water, attach the lid, and shake. If the fibers are evenly distributed in the water, the pulp is ready to use. (Photo 5) Now you're ready to strain and rinse the pulp and add your chosen plant materials. At this point, you can also store the pulp for later use. See "Making Pulp for Storage."

Photo 5 – Testing to see if the pulp is ready.

Photo 4 – Completing the blending.

Continued on next page

▶ *Paper Blending Tips*

• How much paper should you use in your blender?

The basic rule is to allow enough water to provide room for the paper fibers to swell and move away from each other. When working with recycled paper, I start with multiple pieces or one piece of paper that is equal to twice the size I want my finished sheet to be. For example, to make one or two 8½" x 11" sheets of average thickness, I tear five 8½" x 11" sheets or mix several different pieces to equal this amount. I add 3 cups of water to the blender (and may use up to ½ cup more water, depending on the amount of paper.) For smaller size sheets, use less paper and less water.

• Should I soak the paper before using it?

You can soak your papers before blending them for 1 hour or overnight, depending on the thickness. Some papermakers boil recycled papers before blending to remove sizing and other impurities.

• How long to blend?

Because all blenders are not alike, the blending times listed are only guidelines. Keep notes when you first start making papers to learn how your blender behaves with certain fibers and pulp mixtures. Start slowly and observe your pulp as you blend it. A good rule is to blend long enough so that half of the paper fibers are liquefied.

Making the Paper Pulp, continued

Adding an Acid Free Additive

If you wish to include an acid free additive, this is the time to add it. An acid free additive will help avoid bleeding of colors from plant materials and will help prolong the life of your papers. Be sure that you read and follow the supplier's instructions for the correct measurements and to ensure the best results.

Adding Plant Materials

You can use a variety of plant materials or botanicals —leaves, flowers, vegetables, grass, and herbs—to give texture and interest to papers. (Here, it's rose petals.) They can be added to the pulp in the blender or when you form the sheet in the mold. Mixing them with the pulp in the blender allows you to control the density of the particles. Pulse them briefly to retain the plant's visual characteristics and to make a sheet with more texture and variation.

Many natural plant materials will need to be cooked before adding them to the pulp. You will find instructions for cooking the fibers in chapter 3, *Paper Making Recipes.* Chapter 3 gives numerous recipes for using plants and other materials in your sheets.

▶ ADDING COLOR – OPTIONAL

Using the colors in tissue and other recycled papers is the best (and easiest) way to color your pulp. You can also use natural dyes, such as coffees or teas, or vegetables such as beets. Simply brew a strong batch of coffee or tea or use the cooking water from beets and add them to your pulp. Use extra care to protect your tools and supplies. Natural dyes can permanently stain your drying sheets, other tools, and work surfaces.

To tint paper pulp with tissue paper, start by making a batch of white pulp in your blender. Tear some colored tissue paper into 2" squares. Add some of the torn tissue paper pieces to the pulp in the blender. Start with just a few pieces–you can always add more.

Blend the pulp to incorporate the tissue paper and tint the pulp. If the color is not as intense as you'd like, add more tissue until the result pleases you.

Making Pulp for Storage

You can make a large amount of pulp and store it until you are ready to make paper sheets by following these steps. Pulp stored in this way can be used within a few days or stored in the refrigerator for several months. Stored, strained pulp will need to be re-hydrated and lightly blended before using.

You'll Need
• Bowl
• Strainer
• Netting fabric (tulle), cut into 12" squares
• Zipper-top plastic bags *or* airtight plastic storage container(s)

1. Place the strainer over the bowl. Place a piece of tulle inside the strainer to catch the pulp. (Photo 1)
2. Pour the pulp from the blender container into the strainer. Allow the water to drain into the bowl. (Photo 2)
3. When the pulp has drained, lift the tulle (with the pulp inside) with one hand and, with the other hand, squeeze the pulp to remove as much moisture as possible. (Photo 3)
4. Place the damp pulp in a storage container with an airtight lid. (Photo 4)
   TIP: If stored pulp starts developing an odor, mix it with a few drops of bleach and rinse thoroughly before using.

Photo 1

Photo 2

Photo 3

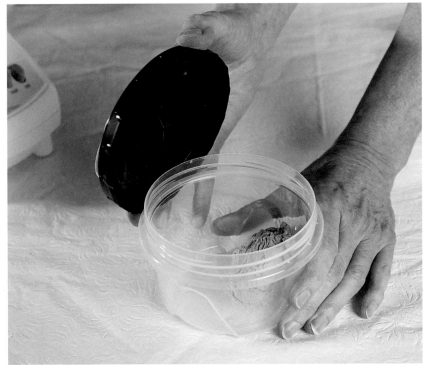

Photo 4

29

ABOUT PH LEVELS

Papers that are pure and pH neutral are considered archival quality. Cellulose is the material in plants that holds paper fibers together. When overly acidic or alkaline materials exist in the pulp, the cellulose will eventually break down and cause the paper to deteriorate. You can use pH test strips to test the acidity and alkalinity of your pulp and your water if you are concerned about longevity. Basically, if the water or pulp pH tests results are over 8.5, the paper will likely deteriorate over time.

Some raw plants and vegetable materials require cooking with an alkaline solution to reduce the pH level of the pulp and extend the life of your finished sheets. (See "Preparing Plant Materials" in the *Paper Making Recipes* section for instructions.) Some plants and vegetables, such as grass, lettuce, carrots, and onions, need only to be cooked in plain water to prepare them for making pulp.

When using purchased or prepared pulps or recycled papers, it's not necessary to cook the pulp, but you should add an acid free additive in the blender to avoid deterioration over time. After your sheets are dry, you can protect them further by spraying or coating them with an acid free sealer.

FORMING SHEETS

The next step is to form the pulp into sheets of paper. You can make free-form or uneven sheets on your mold frame, or you can use a deckle–which is a template that will help you to form sheets with straight edges or into various shapes.

Using a Dip Mold

A dip mold is useful when making multiple sheets of the same kind of paper and when using larger amounts of pulp. The sheets are formed by lifting the mold (and the deckle, if you're using one) out of a vat of water.

1. To get started, assemble your dip mold with the screen attached.
2. Build up your couching surface slightly so that it is almost the same thickness as the sides of your dip mold. To do this, place soft absorbent materials (couch sheets, mesh dishcloths, felt, blankets, towels, or paper towels) on a flat, waterproof tray. Place a couching sheet on materials on the couching tray.
3. Pour your blended paper pulp into the vat. There should be at least 3" of slurry (mixed paper and water) in the vat. (Photo 1)

Photo 1 – Pouring the prepared pulp into the vat.

▶ TIP – When using a dip mold, you'll need to experiment to determine the ratio of pulp to water you'll need to obtain the sheet thickness you want. Using more pulp makes a thicker sheet; removing pulp with a strainer (leaving a higher ratio of water) makes a thinner sheet.

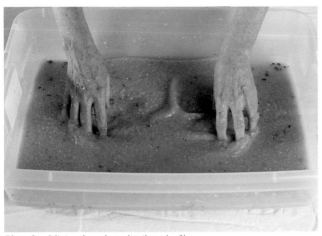

Photo 2 – Mixing the pulp to distribute the fibers.

4. Mix the pulp vigorously with your hands to distribute the fibers, making sure they are suspended in the water, not settled near the bottom. (Photo 2)
5. Run water over your mold before using it the first time so that the pulp will not resist the mold. Dip the mold into the vat at a 45-degree angle and scoop up some of the pulp. (Photo 3)
6. In one smooth movement, position the mold inside the vat as you level it so it's parallel to the bottom of the vat. Pull the mold up out of the vat without stopping. (Photo 4)

Photo 3 – Dipping the mold in the vat.

Photo 4 – Pulling the mold out of the vat.

Continued on next page

Forming Sheets Using a Dip Mold, *continued*

7. Holding the mold level above the vat, allow the water to drain. Shake the mold a little, moving back and forth and left and right (but not too much, or the fibers will shift) as the sheet forms on the screen. Stop shaking when the fibers start to settle on the screen.
8. Place the mold with the wet formed sheet facing the couching sheet. (Photo 5) Turn the mold with the sheet facing down on the couching sheet. (Photo 6)
9. Press down on all of the edges of the mold. Lift one edge of the mold carefully to see if the wet sheet has released from the screen. Carefully lift the mold from the wet sheet. (Photo 7)

Photo 6 – The mold, sheet side down, on the couching tray.

Photo 7 – Lifting the mold from the sheet.

Photo 5 – Positioning the mold at the edge of the couching sheet.

Proceed to "Couching."

See instructions for couching on page 36.

▶ *Cleaning the Mold*

To remove pulp from a dip mold, first remove the deckle if you are using one. Flip the mold over and smack the mold on the surface of the water. The pulp will fall into the water and your mold will be clean. This is called *kissing off*. Stir the vat and adjust your pulp mixture before making another sheet.

Photo 1 – Placing the mold in the water.

Photo 2 – Adding the paper pulp.

Using a Pour Mold

When using a pour mold you submerge the mold in a vat of water and pour the blended pulp into the mold. The sides of a pour mold are deeper than the sides of a dip mold. A pour mold is most useful when working with smaller amounts of pulp or when combining different pulps together to form a single sheet.

The pour mold I like best came in a paper making kit. It is constructed with hook-and-loop tape straps that allow the bottom screen (and the deckle, if you're using one) to be separated easily from the mold with the wet paper sheet positioned on the screen. This makes couching much easier.

1. To get started, assemble the mold, following the manufacturer's instructions. Place the mold upside down on a flat surface and pull the straps across the drain rack as tightly as you can. Turn the mold right side up.
2. Holding the mold at a slight angle, lower it into the water in the vat or tub. (Photo 1) When the mold is resting on the bottom, there should be 2" to 3" of water in the mold. Add more water, if needed, until the water is at the proper depth.
3. Pour the prepared pulp into the mold. (Photo 2)
4. Use your fingers to mix the paper pulp with the water standing inside the mold. (Photo 3)

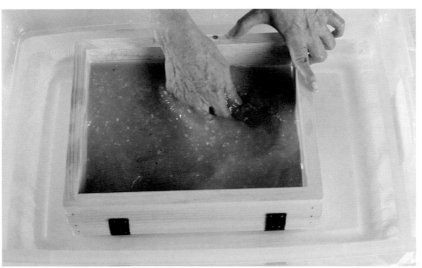

Photo 3 – Mixing the pulp with the water in the mold.

Continued on next page

Forming Sheets Using a Pour Mold, *continued*

Photo 4 – Lifting the mold from the water.

5. Lift the mold out of the water, holding it level and allowing the water to drain. Gently shake the mold back and forth and left and right as the sheet forms on the surface of the screen. Be careful not to shake too much. Stop shaking when the fibers are starting to settle on the screen. (Photo 4)
6. Place the mold on a waterproof tray and loosen the straps. Lift the mold away from the screen and drain rack inside the tray. Set the mold aside. (Photo 5)
7. Place the gray cover screen over the new sheet. (Photo 6)
8. Press the sponge firmly over the gray cover screen to absorb water from the paper pulp. Wring out the sponge when it gets full of water. Continue pressing the sponge over different areas of the paper sheet and wringing out the sponge until you've blotted as much water as you can (when the sponge is no longer absorbing water). (Photo 7)

Photo 5 – Removing mold from formed sheet.

Photo 6 – Placing cover screen on formed sheet.

Photo 7 – Pressing water from sheet.

▶ Cleaning the Mold

To remove wet pulp from a pour mold, very slowly lower the mold at a slight angle back into the water in the vat. Mix the pulp with your fingers and make adjustments to the pulp mixture before making the next sheet.

Photo 8 – Lifting the screen.

Photo 9 – Pressing water from formed sheet.

9. Carefully lift one corner of the gray cover screen from the paper slowly and peel up the cover screen. Set it aside. (Photo 8)

10. Prepare a hard surface with a couch sheet on top of it. Pick up the white papermaking screen with the newly formed paper sheet on it. Turn it over and place it on top of a dry couch sheet so that the new paper sheet is between the white papermaking screen and the couch sheet. Press the sponge firmly on top of the white papermaking screen to pick up water from the paper. Wring out the sponge as needed. Continue pressing the sponge over the screen and wringing it out until the sponge will absorb no more water. (photo 9)

11. To remove the papermaking screen, place one hand near the middle and one hand at the corner of the screen and lift the corner. Continue lifting the screen while you slowly move the other hand back, revealing the paper sheet. (Photo 10) TIP: If the sheet sticks to the screen, start with another corner.

▶ Finish the process by proceeding to the instructions for *Couching*. You can also use a deckle in a dip mold–if you do, lay the deckle on top of the mold, put the white papermaking screen on top of the deckle, and the drain rack on top of the screen when assembling the mold. *See instructions for using a deckle later in this chapter.*

Photo 10 – A formed sheet ready to be couched.

COUCHING

The term couch (which rhymes with "pooch") comes from the French verb *coucher,* which means "to lay down." Couching is the process of using a sponge and dishcloths, felts, blankets, blotter paper, or couching sheets to remove water from the formed sheet of paper. The process of wringing the sponge, flipping the sheets, and replacing wet couch sheets with dry ones is repeated until the paper sheet is damp, not wet, and all the water that can be removed by couching has been removed.

1. Put a dry couch sheet on top of the wet paper sheet. (Photo 1)
2. Press a sponge firmly over the top of the couch sheet, allowing it to soak up water. (Photo 2) Wring out the sponge. Continue pressing the sponge on all parts of the sheet to remove water and wringing out the sponge until no more water is absorbed by the sponge.
3. Place one hand near the middle of the couch sheet and one hand at one corner. Lift the corner while moving the other hand back. Remove the wet couch sheet. TIP: If the paper sheet does not separate from the couch sheet, try another corner.
4. Put a dry couch sheet over the paper sheet. Use a wooden press bar (Photo 3) or a roller (Photo 4) to press down on the couch sheet. Continue rolling or pressing on all parts of the couch sheet to flatten the paper sheet and press out more water.
5. Remove the top couching sheet. (Photo 5)
6. Pick up the bottom couch sheet with the paper sheet on top.
7. Carefully turn the paper sheet onto a dishcloth or other absorbent cloth and gently peel away the couch sheet. (Photo 6)

▶ You are now ready to proceed to the *Pressing and Drying* stage. There are a variety of options for drying the paper sheets.

Photo 1 – Placing a dry couch sheet on top.

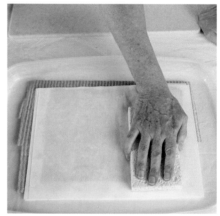

Photo 2 – Using a sponge to remove water.

▶ TIP – Always clean your mold, deckle, and vat or tub after each use and place them on a level surface to dry. Rinse your couch sheets after each use to remove excess pulp and allow them to dry. Clean cooking pots and utensils after each use. Recycled paper materials contain a lot of ink and processing chemicals that can leave residues, which eventually build up on your tools if you don't clean them regularly.

Photo 3 – Using a wooden press bar to remove water.

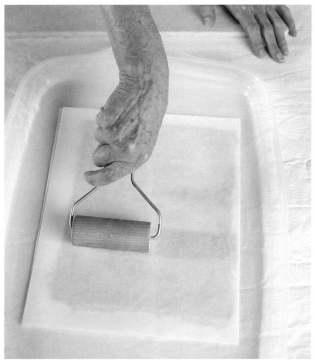

Photo 4 – Using a roller to remove water.

Photo 5 – Removing the top couching sheet.

Photo 6 – Peeling away the couch sheet from the new paper sheet.

PRESSING & DRYING

There are a number of options you can choose for drying your paper sheets. When allowed to dry naturally, paper sheets will curl and buckle. To make smoother, flatter sheets, use an iron or a paper press. Presses will push the wet fibers closer together, resulting in a stronger sheet of paper.

Ironing: Option 1

Ironing sheets of damp (already couched) paper will speed the drying time considerably. The iron will flatten and compress the paper; the heat will evaporate moisture. When ironing, work on a heatproof board to protect your work surface, and place a dry mesh dishcloth (or other thin cloth) under the paper sheet.

1. Cover the paper sheet with another dry dishcloth (or other thin cloth), using it like a pressing cloth.
2. Using a dry iron set medium to hot, move the iron continuously over the sheet. (Photo 1) The dishcloths will absorb moisture; swap wet ones for dry ones frequently. TIP: An iron with a non-stick soleplate works best–some paper additives might stick to the hot iron.

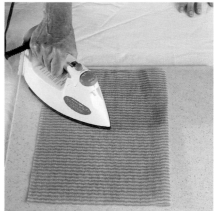
Photo 1 – Pressing the paper sheet with an iron.

Using a Homemade Paper Press: Option 2

You can make a simple homemade press by layering damp paper sheets between dry couch sheets and positioning them between two pieces of polyurethane-coated wood. The sheets and wood are pressed together with c-clamps. (Photo 2)

Pressing sheets in a homemade press is done just the same as when using a professional press. Place each damp, couched sheet between two dry couch sheets. After 20 minutes, swap those couch sheets for dry ones. Replace the couch sheets again after a few hours. Leave the paper in the press overnight for best results. Thicker sheets may require additional drying after they are removed from the press.

Photo 2 – A homemade drying press.

Using a Professional Paper Press: Option 3

Professional paper presses speed drying time and create beautiful, flat, even sheets of paper. (Photo 3) The pressure they provide helps compress the fibers, creating a denser, stronger bond that produces a higher quality, more durable sheet of paper. To press sheets in a purchased press, place each damp, couched sheet between two dry couch sheets. After 20 minutes, swap those couch sheets for dry ones. Replace the couch sheets again after a few hours. Leave the paper in the press overnight for best results. Thicker sheets may require additional drying after they are removed from the press.

Photo 3 – A purchased paper press.

Photo 4 – Drying a paper sheet on a wire rack.

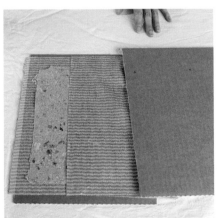

Photo 5 – Layering paper, dishcloths, and cardboard to make a microwave press.

Photo 6 – The microwave press secured with rubber bands.

Air Drying: Option 4

Wire racks allow air to circulate around the wet sheets of paper (Photo 4), producing a more textured paper that won't be completely flat. (The paper will curl naturally but will flatten if glued to a flat surface.) Allow 24 hours for air drying thinner sheets, longer for thicker sheets.

Using a Microwave: Option 5

You can use a simple homemade press in your microwave to speed paper pressing and drying. (Online and mail order outlets sell microwave flower presses that can be used for drying small sheets of paper.)

1. Place sheets of damp, couched paper between four dry paper towels or dishcloths and put them between two pieces of cardboard. (Photo 5)
2. Secure the layered cardboard, papers, and paper towels with two rubber bands. (Photo 6)
3. Remove the rotating ring from your microwave (if you have one) and turn the glass platter upside down in the center of the microwave so it will elevate the cardboard press.
4. For best results, dry everything in multiple stages. After each stage, wait a few seconds to let the paper cool. Then remove the rubber bands and check the dried materials before proceeding. The first stage will be the longest, followed by multiple shorter ones. Use the high setting on your microwave and refer to the *Microwave Drying Chart* times for the stages.

With practice you will discover what works best for your microwave. Other factors that affect drying times are the thickness and dampness of the papers. Either could add time to the process.

MICROWAVE DRYING CHART

MICROWAVE WATTAGE	600 OR LOWER	750	950 OR HIGHER
First cycle	45 seconds	30 seconds	20 seconds
Second cycle	23 seconds	15 seconds	10 seconds
Additional cycles	5-10 seconds	5-10 seconds	5 seconds

USING A DECKLE

A deckle is a template or form used to make special sizes and shapes of paper. The paper pulp will settle inside the deckle, forming a specific paper shape or size. You can use a deckle with a dip mold or a pour mold. We show it here with a dip mold.

Step 1: Position the deckle on the dip mold and hold the deckle in place with your thumbs as you dip the mold into the vat.

Step 2: Lift the mold from the vat, still holding the deckle in place.

Step 3: Carefully lift the deckle off the mold.

Step 4: The shaped paper pieces are ready to be placed on couching sheets to dry. Proceed to *Couching* then *Pressing & Drying*.

EMBEDDING DRIED FLOWERS

Dried flowers, petals, and leaves can be easily added to wet pulp sheets before couching. These embedded materials make beautiful sheets of paper with extra depth and dimension. Simply place the materials you want to embed on a wet pulp sheet and partially cover them with more pulp. The materials will join with the paper as it dries. You can also embed other items such as different colors of pulps, threads, lace, or fibers.

Step 1: Place individual flower petals on a wet pulp sheet.

Step 2: Add a little wet pulp around each petal, then couch the sheet, press, and dry.

▶ LAMINATING

This is another creative technique to try. Couch two wet sheets of pulp together with dried, pressed materials between the sheets–called laminating. See "Layered Herb Paper" and "Laminated Lavender Paper" in the *Paper Making Recipes* section for instructions.

Paper with embedded rose petals.

ADDING TEXTURE

You can use simple everyday items in your home to make textured imprints in your papers, including bricks, burlap, fabrics, wood, foam, wire, baskets, the soles of your shoes, doilies, rugs, bubble wrap, and leaves. Simply cover a couched paper sheet with an item that has a raised pattern to make impressions in the paper. Allow to dry with the item in place, then remove. Here, two straw placemats are used to create a textured paper sheet.

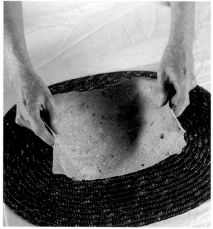

Step 1: Position a couched paper sheet on one placemat.

A paper sheet with imprint of the straw placemats.

Step 2: Put the other placemat on top of the paper sheet and press with your hands. Allow to dry.

The texture on this paper sheet was created by pressing a rubber stamp into the center of the couched sheet.

A paper sheet with texture created by laying a brick on the paper while it was drying.

COLORING

Adding color to your sheets can be done with a variety of mediums. The color is added during the pulp making process. See *Adding Color* in the section entitled *Making the Paper Pulp* for more details.

This blue paper was made by adding dye to the pulp.

Pink fabric dye was added to the pulp to create this color

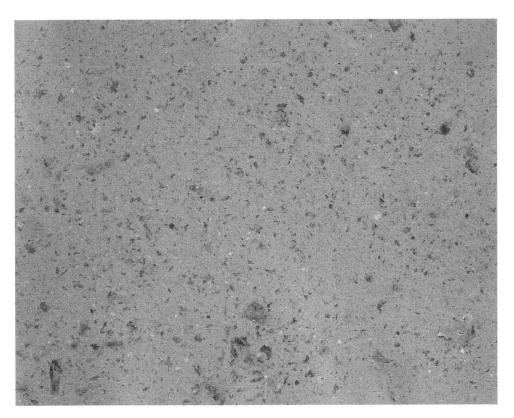

Tissue paper was blended with the pulp to create the orange color.

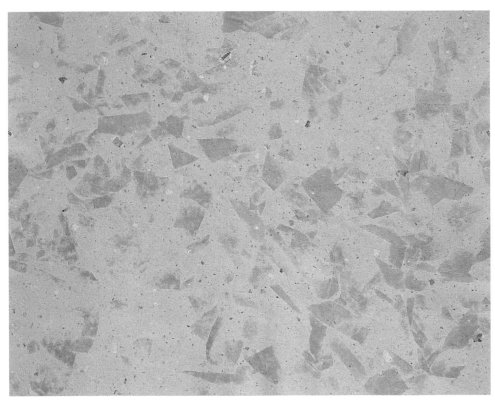

Green tissue paper was blended just slightly with the pulp. The pulp was blended, then tissue paper was added and allowed to stay in larger pieces.

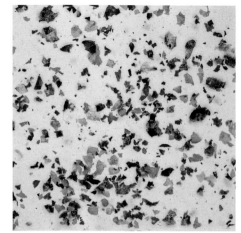

Chapter

3.

PAPER MAKING RECIPES

This section includes recipes for making more than 25 types of handmade papers, plus a wealth of recipe variations and numerous photos. The lists of ingredients include the prepared recycled pulp from the Paper Making Process section. The amount of recycled pulp included in the recipes is based on using previously blended and strained pulp. Water is added to the blender and the pulp is re-hydrated by blending. Each recipe should make one or two sheets of 8½" x 11" paper, depending on thickness—to make thicker sheets add more pulp; to make thinner sheets add more water. A comprehensive list of plants to use for paper making appears at the end of the recipes.

As you work, keep in mind that making paper with natural materials is not an exact science. Even if you measure carefully, it is almost impossible to get the same results twice. Sit back, take your time, relax, and enjoy the unpredictable results that appear with each new sheet. There is no single right way to make a sheet of paper.

After trying these recipes, I hope you will experiment with different materials and learn how they respond to each other. With time and practice, you will learn the best ways to incorporate your favorite plant materials in papers and develop a style of your own.

PREPARING PLANT MATERIALS

Gathering and preparing plant materials takes work, ingenuity, and some experimentation. Many natural plant materials need to be cooked before adding them to your pulp. The recipes in this chapter will give specific instructions for cooking.

Materials such as grass clippings from your lawn, rhubarb stalks, lettuce leaves, onion skins, beets, kiwi fruit, and carrot tops can be cooked in plain water and added to your paper recipes. The fibers in more dense plant parts, such as thick leaves or stalks, will break down faster if they are cooked in an alkaline solution. You can mix a solution with water and soda ash, washing soda, or fireplace ashes. For instructions for making a fireplace ash solution, see the Paper Making Supplies section.

▶ COOKING WITH SODA ASH OR WASHING SODA

Option #1:
Add $1/2$ ounce or 1 tablespoon of *either* soda ash *or* washing soda to each quart of water.

Option #2:
Measure $3^{1}/_{2}$ oz. for each pound of dry fibers and add water to cover.

▶ COOKING WITH FIREPLACE ASH SOLUTION

Option #1: Use 1 oz. or 2 tablespoons of fireplace ash solution.

Option #2: Measure 7 oz. for each pound of dry fibers. Add water to cover.

SAFETY TIPS FOR COOKING WITH ALKALINE SOLUTIONS

• Cook outside, if possible.

• Wear gloves and a mask to protect yourself from accidental splashes.

• Use stainless steel, enamel-coated, or glass pots and stainless steel or wooden spoons and other utensils. Never use aluminum, tin, or iron pots or utensils–they can react chemically with the alkaline solutions and produce a toxic gas.

• Don't use the pots or utensils you use for preparing plant materials for cooking food. Store them separately, out of the kitchen.

• Add the alkaline solution to the water before it boils; add plant materials after the solution is dissolved.

• Never add more water to the boiling solution–it could cause a chemical reaction and result in uncontrolled splattering.

IVY LEAF PAPER

Use this recipe to add ivy leaves or almost any green or dried leaves to a recycled pulp mixture. Cooking in an alkaline solution will break down the leaf fibers and produce a strong paper with a lot of embedded leaf material.

The leaves must be rinsed well before making the sheets. Be sure the rinse water runs clear before you add the cooked leaves to the blender to prolong the life of your paper. The result is worth the effort—you'll have brilliant, earth-toned sheets.

When gathering leaves for paper making, always collect twice as many as you think you will need. Cooking shrinks them considerably.

▶ What If I Want to Cook More Leaves?

When cooking more than 1 cup of torn leaves:
1. Tear the leaves, place them in a pot, and cover with water.
2. Drain and measure the amount of water used.
3. Add approximately $1/2$ oz. (or 1 tablespoon) of soda ash or washing soda for each quart used. Or use 1 oz. (or 2 tablespoons) of fireplace ash solution for each quart of water used.

▶ RECIPE

INGREDIENTS

1 cup torn ivy or other leaves

2 oz. soda ash *or* 4 oz. fireplace ash solution

1 cup prepared and strained recycled paper pulp

Acid free additive

TOOLS

Large non-reactive pot and spoon (stainless steel, enamel-coated, or glass)

Large strainer

Stovetop *or* hot plate

Blender

INSTRUCTIONS

1. Soak the leaves in water overnight. Put them in a strainer and rinse.
2. Fill the pot with water and heat the water.
3. Before the water boils, add the soda ash or fireplace ash solution and stir until it dissolves. Bring the water to a boil.
4. Tear the leaves into 1" pieces. Carefully put them in the boiling water.
5. Reduce the heat to a simmer and cook for about 2 hours, stirring every 30 minutes. Remove from heat. Drain.
6. Rinse the leaves several times until the water runs clear. This step removes the alkaline solution. It will take about one hour.
7. Add the recycled paper pulp and acid free additive to the blender. (Follow the package instructions for how much additive to use.) Add water to the blender until it is about three-quarters full.
8. Blend for 30 seconds.
9. Add the leaves to the blender and pulse for 2 to 3 seconds to process.
10. Follow the steps in The Paper Making Process section to make your paper.

49

GRASS PAPER

Use this recipe for adding grass clippings. You can also get the same look by adding other thin leafy materials such as carrot tops to recycled pulp. You don't need to make an alkaline solution to cook thin grasses or leaves–they decompose more easily than thicker plant materials.

▶ How to Add More Color

To add more color to your papers, save the water from the cooking process and add it to the blender instead of using clear water. This will very lightly tint the pulp.

Grass Paper

INGREDIENTS

1 cup grass clippings or dried
   carrot tops

1 cup prepared and strained
   recycled paper pulp

Acid free additive

TOOLS

Large non-reactive pot and
   spoon (stainless steel,
   enamel-coated, or glass)

Large strainer

Stovetop *or* hot plate

Blender

INSTRUCTIONS

1. Put the grass, carrot tops, or thin leaves in the pot. Fill the pot with enough water to cover the plant materials completely. Bring to a boil.

2. Reduce the heat to a simmer and continue cooking for 1 hour, stirring after 30 minutes.

3. Drain, reserving the water (See *How to Add More Color*) and rinse the cooked plant materials. They will rinse clean very quickly.

4. Add the recycled paper pulp and acid free additive to the blender. (Follow the package instructions for how much additive to use.) Add the reserved cooking water to the blender until it is about three-quarters full.

5. Blend for 30 seconds.

6. Add the cooked plant materials and pulse for 2 to 3 seconds until the clippings are processed.

7. Follow the steps in The Paper Making Process section to make your paper.

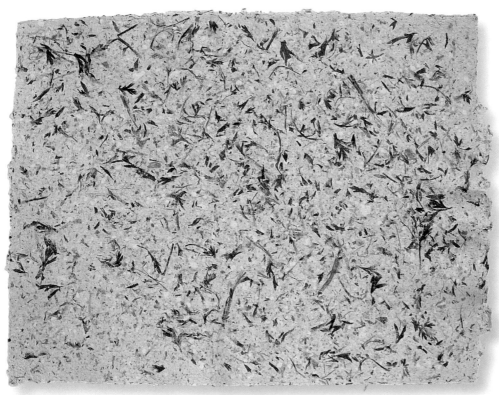

Carrot Tops Paper

ONION & GARLIC SKIN PAPER

The skins and fibers of onions and garlic give papers personality, texture, and interest, and the natural plant pigments from onion skins can produce very subtle shades in papers. When boiled, the plant materials create a concentrated liquid that can be used to stain (add color to) the pulp. Purchased cotton pulp will take the stain much better than recycled pulps. For a deeper tint, allow the liquid pulp to sit for 4 to 6 hours or overnight before using it to make paper sheets.

▶ Variation

For the garlic skins, cooking the skins gives a more transparent look to the paper; uncooked skins retain more of their natural appearance and texture. When I made the garlic paper, I mixed cooked and uncooked skins. The garlic skins are less visible if you use a light color of recycled paper pulp; they are more visible if you use darker-colored recycled paper.

Grass Paper

▶ RECIPE

INGREDIENTS

1 cup chopped onion or
    garlic skins

1 cup prepared and strained
    paper pulp

Acid free additive

TOOLS

Large non-reactive pot and
    spoon (stainless steel,
    enamel-coated, or glass)

Large strainer

Stovetop *or* hot plate

INSTRUCTIONS

1. Put the onion skin pieces in the pot and fill it with enough water to cover the plant materials. Bring to a boil. *When I made the garlic paper, I only cooked half of the garlic skins.*

2. Reduce the heat to a simmer and continue cooking for 1 hour, stirring after 30 minutes.

3. Drain and rinse the cooked skins or leaves, reserving the cooked liquid.

4. Add the paper pulp and acid free additive to the blender. (Follow the package instructions regarding how much additive to use.)

5. Add the reserved liquid to the blender until the container is three-quarters full. Add water if necessary.

6. Blend for 30 seconds.

7. Add the cooked skins (and uncooked skins) to the blender and pulse for 2 to 3 seconds.

8. Follow the steps in The Paper Making Process section to make your paper.

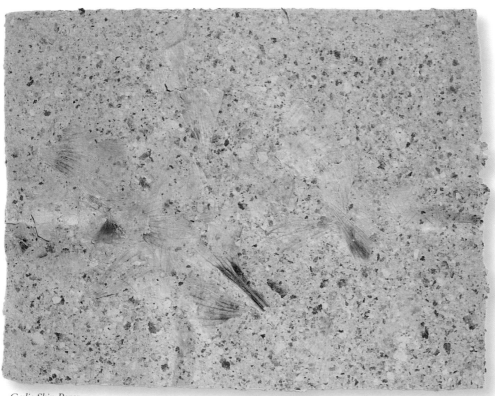

Garlic Skin Paper

COFFEE & TEA PAPER

Coffee and tea can be used to make beautiful tinted papers. For added texture, you can add coffee grounds or tea leaves to the blender when blending the pulps. For best results, make a strong tea or coffee mixture and soak the pulp for several hours before proceeding. Because of the high acid levels in coffee and tea, always use an acid free additive to protect these papers from age and exposure.

Coffee Paper made with coffee grounds.

INGREDIENTS

8 tea bags *or* 8 tablespoons ground coffee

3 cups water

1 cup prepared and strained recycled paper pulp

Acid free additive

TOOLS

Kettle

Teapot *or* coffee pot *or* 4 cup glass measuring cup

Stovetop *or* hot plate

INSTRUCTIONS

1. Boil 3 cups of water.
2. Add the tea bags or ground coffee to the teapot, coffee pot, or glass measuring cup. Pour in the boiling water. Steep at least 30 minutes and let cool.
3. *If using tea,* squeeze the tea bags to get all of the color from them. *If using coffee,* strain, reserving the grounds.
4. Add the recycled paper pulp and acid free additive to the blender container. Follow the package instructions regarding how much additive to use. Add tea or coffee water until the blender container is three-quarters full. For added texture, add some coffee grounds or tea leaves.
5. Blend for 30 seconds.
6. Allow the liquid pulp to soak for 4 to 6 hours or overnight to absorb the coffee or tea colors.
7. Follow the steps in The Paper Making Process section to make your paper.

Tea Paper made without tea leaves.

FLOWER PETAL PAPER

Dried flower petals make beautiful and colorful papers. For best results, use the freshest, most colorful dried flowers available to get the best color retention. You can dry the petals by pressing or using a desiccant. While almost all flowers or petals fade over time, the process can be delayed by spraying or coating them with surface sealers and avoiding exposure to direct light, heat, humidity, or extreme hot or cold temperatures. Some dried flower petals, such as marigolds and carnations, hold their color better than roses. Purchased cotton pulps will make a brighter sheet of paper than recycled pulp. More delicate petals look better when mixed with cotton pulp.

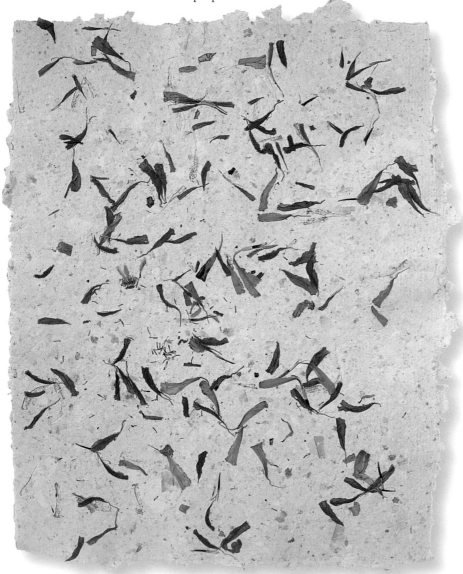

▶ To bleed or not to bleed?

Dried flower petals can bleed color into the surrounding paper or they may fade in color. Deep red flowers may turn blue; yellow and white flower petals may turn brown; pink will possibly lose all of its color. While no method will guarantee that dried flowers will not bleed or fade, here are some suggestions for preserving color:

• To reduce color bleeding with roses, spray them with a fixative and add an acid free additive to your pulp mixture.

• Blanching dried flowers for about 5 minutes in boiling water will help to retain more color and avoid bleeding. However, blanching may alter the flower's color.

• Instead of stopping the bleeding process, consider encouraging it to naturally occur by mixing the pulp and flower petals with water and allowing them to steep for 5 minutes or longer before making your sheets.

INGREDIENTS

½ cup crushed dried rose petals *or* other dried flower petals

1 cup prepared and strained paper pulp

Spray fixative

Sizing or acid free additive

INSTRUCTIONS

1. To avoid bleeding, spray the petals with fixative and allow them to dry *or* blanch them for 5 minutes in boiling water. Drain and allow them to cool completely.

2. Add the pulp and sizing or acid free additive to the blender container. Follow the package instructions regarding how much sizing or additive to use. Add water to the container until it is three-quarters full.

3. Blend for 30 seconds.

4. Add the petals. Here are three options:
   - Add the petals to the blender and pulse for 2 to 3 seconds.
   - To retain the natural look of the petals in the finished sheet (and to avoid over-blending), add the blanched petals to the pulp after you've poured it into the mold rather than adding them to the blender. Stir them into the pulp inside the mold with a whisk or your fingers.
   - Add some of the blanched petals to the blender and blend; add the rest to the mold and stir.

5. Follow the steps in The Paper Making Process section to make your paper.

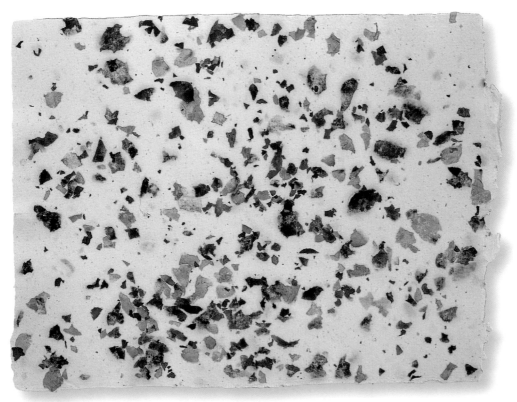

Rose Petal Paper

SEED PAPER

It is very easy to make paper with embedded seeds that can be planted. Small flat seeds like those of forget-me-not, hollyhock, lavender, chili pepper, and tomato work wonderfully. Be sure to stir the mixture in the vat or mold before making sheets to ensure even seed distribution. The sheet shown on the opposite page contains sunflower seeds.

▶ RECIPE

INGREDIENTS

½ cup flat flower seeds *or* vegetable seeds

1 cup prepared and strained recycled paper pulp

Acid free additive

INSTRUCTIONS

1. Put the paper pulp and acid free additive in the blender container. See the package instructions regarding how much additive to use. Add water until the container is about three-quarters full.

2. Blend for 30 seconds.

3. Add the seeds to the blender and pulse for 2 to 3 seconds *or* add them to the pulp after pouring it in the mold and stir the seeds into the pulp with a whisk or your fingers.

4. Follow the steps in The Paper Making Process section to make your paper.

Include these instructions with your gift of plantable seed papers.

PLANTING INSTRUCTIONS

Plant in the Ground
Tear off bits of paper that contain seeds and plant directly in the ground. The paper will compost naturally.

Sprouting the Seeds Before Planting
To sprout the seeds before planting, dampen the paper and put it in a plastic bag. Check periodically to be sure the paper stays moist. Keep the plastic bag at room temperature until the seeds sprout, then transplant them to pots or directly in the garden.

DENIM PAPER

Paper can be made with almost any kind of fabric, lace, or burlap using this recipe. (Now you have a use for all of those tiny little fabric swatches that you have been saving!) Fabric paper is also known as rag paper. The beautiful paper can be quickly dried with an iron. This recipe was developed from a recipe created by Patty Cox.

Photo 1 – Soaking the paper and fabric pieces.

▶ RECIPE

INGREDIENTS

1 cup denim fabric or other fabric

5 sheets recycled paper,
    each 8½" x 11"

TOOLS

Scissors

Bowl *or* bucket

Blender

INSTRUCTIONS

1. Cut the denim or other fabric into ½" pieces. Tear the recycled paper into 2" pieces. Put the fabric and paper pieces in a bowl or bucket.

2. Fill the bowl or bucket with enough water to cover the pieces of fabric and paper. Allow to soak overnight. (Photo 1)

3. Squeeze the water out of one handful of the soaked fabric and paper mixture and form it into a 2" ball.

4. Put the ball in the blender container. (Photo 2) Add water to the container until it is three-quarters full.

5. Blend on medium to high speed for 30 seconds or more. (Photo 3)
   Note: If you hear the blender straining, stop it immediately and check the blades to see if threads from the fabric have wrapped around them. Remove any clumps of threads and continue blending.

6. If the pulp is not evenly blended after one minute, use your fingers to remove any clumps of threads that haven't blended and add more fabric and pulp. Keep blending and removing clumps until the pulp is evenly blended and smooth.

7. Follow the steps in The Paper Making Process section to make your paper. Store leftover pulp in airtight containers in the refrigerator for later use.

Photo 2 – Putting a ball of pulp in the blender.

Photo 3 – Blending the pulp with water.

61

HERB PAPER

Dried and fresh herbs make very fragrant papers, but the scent will not last long. Try rosemary, thyme, basil, parsley, oregano, or dill. You can also add powdered spices (paprika, tumeric, curry powder, saffron or chili powder) and seeds (sesame seeds, poppy seeds, celery seeds) for texture and color.

▶ Variation: Layered Herb Paper

Herb stems and sprigs can be laminated between two couched sheets. Here's how:

1. Make a sheet of paper and couch it.
2. Arrange the stems or sprigs on top.
3. Make another sheet of the same paper. Couch it on top of the first sheet with the stems or sprigs.
4. Press and peel back portions of the laminated sheets to reveal the shapes of the stems and sprigs.

Rosemary Paper made with fresh rosemary.

▶ RECIPE

INGREDIENTS

4 tablespoons dried herbs *and/or* ¼ to ½ cup fresh herbs (depending on the look you desire)

1 cup prepared and strained recycled paper pulp

INSTRUCTIONS

1. Place the recycled paper pulp in the blender container. Add water until the container is about three-quarters full.
2. Blend for 30 seconds.
3. Pull the leaves off the mint stems and put them in the blender.
4. Pulse for 2 to 3 seconds to distribute the leaves.
5. Follow the steps in The Paper Making Process section to make your paper. *Option:* If you want larger leaf pieces in your paper, prepare the pulp and pour it into the mold, then add leaves to the pulp in the mold. Use a whisk or your fingers to mix the leaves with the pulp before making the sheet.

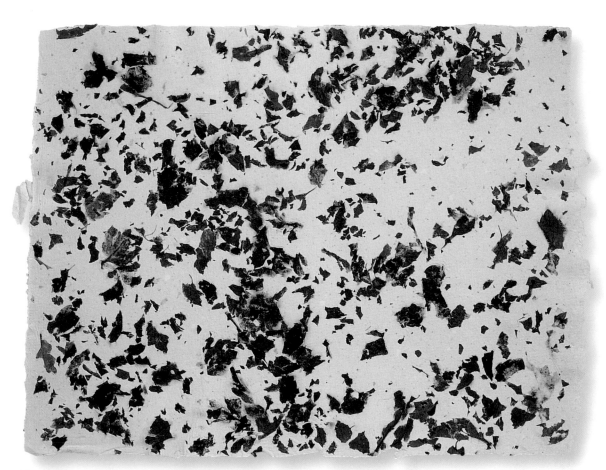

Mint Paper made with fresh mint.

MOSS PAPER

Moss makes a beautiful pale green or gray paper with textured specks of natural material. Fresh moss will result in a yellow paper, while dried Spanish or reindeer moss will retain its color and add a pale color and a natural texture to your papers. Experiment with mixing the different colors and types of mosses together to achieve some surprisingly colorful results.

Spanish moss

▶ RECIPE

INGREDIENTS

½ cup Spanish moss *or* fresh moss
    or reindeer moss

1 cup prepared and strained
    recycled paper pulp

INSTRUCTIONS

1. Put the recycled paper pulp in the blender container. Add water until the container is about three-quarters full.

2. Blend for 30 seconds.

3. Tear the moss into 1" pieces. Add the moss pieces to the blender.

4. Pulse for 2 to 3 seconds to distribute the moss.

5. Follow the steps in The Paper Making Process section to make your paper.

Reindeer moss

▶ TIP – For beautiful variations, combine moss with flower petals, herbs, and leaves to make gorgeous papers.

LAVENDER PAPER

Lavender paper makes a fragrant liner for shelves and drawers. You can use dried buds, dried leaves, or fresh leaves to make the paper.

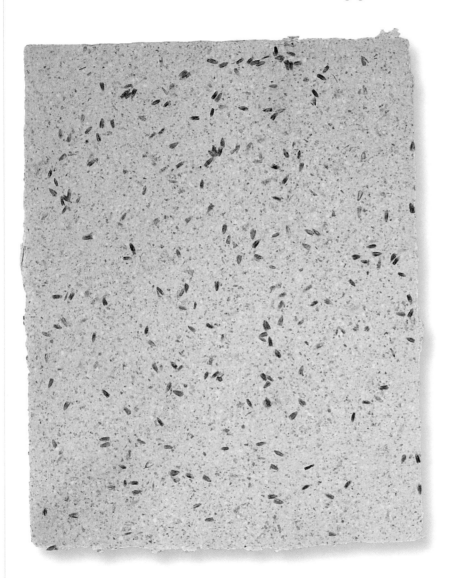

RECIPE

INGREDIENTS

2 tablespoons dried lavender buds *or* fresh lavender leaves

1 cup prepared and strained recycled paper pulp

INSTRUCTIONS

1. Place the recycled paper pulp in the blender container. Add water until the container is about three-quarters full.
2. Blend for 30 seconds.
3. Remove the leaves from the fresh lavender stems and place them in the blender *or* add the dried lavender buds to the blender.
4. Pulse 2 to 3 seconds to distribute the leaves or buds.
5. Follow the steps in The Paper Making Process section to make your paper.

QUEEN ANNE'S LACE PAPER

Queen Anne's lace grows wild in many areas; look along the roadsides in late summer—you may be surprised to find an abundant supply. Dried Queen Anne's lace flowers make a beautiful textured paper. You only need five small dried flower heads to make one sheet.

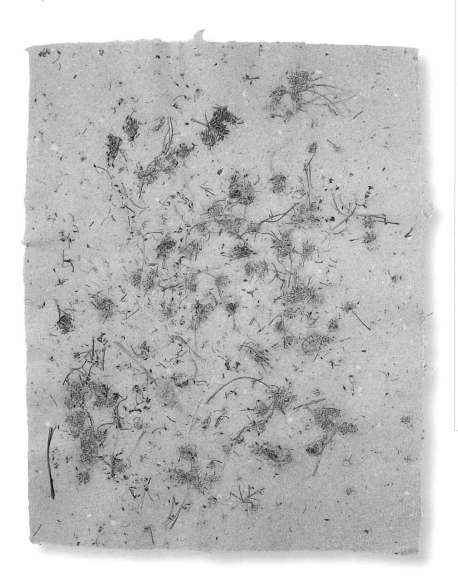

▶ RECIPE

INGREDIENTS

5 Queen Anne's lace flower heads

1 cup prepared and strained recycled paper pulp

Acid free additive

INSTRUCTIONS

1. Add the pulp and acid free additive to the blender container. Follow the package instructions regarding how much additive to use. Add water to the container until it is three-quarters full.
2. Blend for 30 seconds.
3. Pour the pulp into the mold and add the flower heads to the pulp.
4. Stir the pulp very gently—only one time—with your fingers.
5. Follow the steps in The Paper Making Process section to make your paper.

FERN PAPER

Ferns are some of the most widely used plants in paper making—use varieties available in your garden or from your local nursery to give your papers a personal touch.

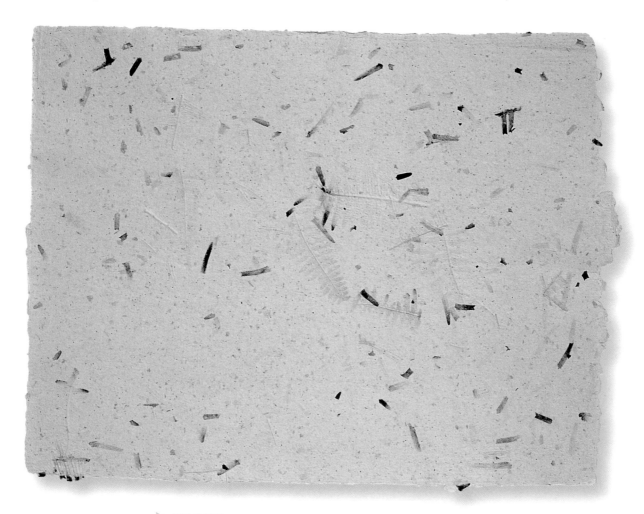

▶ RECIPE

INGREDIENTS

½ cup fern fronds, with woody stems removed

1 cup prepared and strained recycled paper pulp

INSTRUCTIONS

1. Place the recycled paper pulp in the blender container. Add water until the container is three-quarters full.

2. Blend for 30 seconds.

3. Add the fern fronds to the blender.

4. Pulse 2 to 3 seconds.

5. Follow the steps in The Paper Making Process section to make your paper.

JUNIPER PAPER

Small juniper needles as well as cedar needles add natural, rustic inter-est and texture. Experiment with combinations of ferns, junipers, and cedars with flowers and leaves to create unique papers.

▶ RECIPE

INGREDIENTS

½ cup juniper needles *or* cedar needles, with tough stems removed

1 cup prepared and strained recycled paper pulp

INSTRUCTIONS

1. Place the recycled paper pulp in the blender container. Add water until the container is three-quarters full.

2. Blend for 30 seconds.

3. Add the juniper or cedar to the blender.

4. Pulse for 2 to 3 seconds.

5. Follow the steps in The Paper Making Process section to make your paper.

SOY FIBERS PAPER

Soy fibers are silky byproducts of manufacturing processes that create a wide variety of soy-based products. You may need scissors to cut the fibers—they are very strong and cannot be easily torn. They make very strong, durable sheets of paper.

Soy fibers can be found where paper making supplies are sold. Dyed soy fibers create rich, vibrant colors. The fibers can also be found in their natural, neutral, cream-colored state. Papers made with them resemble tie-dyed patterns from the 1960s.

Photo 1 – Natural and dyed soy fibers.

▶ RECIPE

INGREDIENTS

1 cup soy fibers (See Photo 1.)

1 cup prepared and strained recycled paper pulp

TOOLS

Blender

Scissors

Optional: Whisk

INSTRUCTIONS

1. Prepare the dry soy fibers by separating them and arranging them on a flat surface. (Photo 2) The fibers tend to stick together and are difficult to separate when wet.

2. Put the recycled paper pulp in the blender. Add water until the blender container is three-quarters full.

3. Blend for 30 seconds.

4. Pour the pulp into a mold. Add the soy fibers to the pulp inside the mold. Use your fingers or a whisk to move the fibers around until they are evenly distributed. (Photo 3)

5. Leave the soy fibers in the mold to release the dye colors. Dyed soy fibers bleed, and the longer you leave them in the water inside the mold, the more they will bleed.

6. Follow the steps in The Paper Making Process section to make your paper. When your sheets are dry, carefully rub your finger across the grain of the papers. The fibers will release and produce gorgeous, deep colors.

Photo 2 – Separating and arranging the fibers.

Photo 3 – The fibers arranged in the mold.

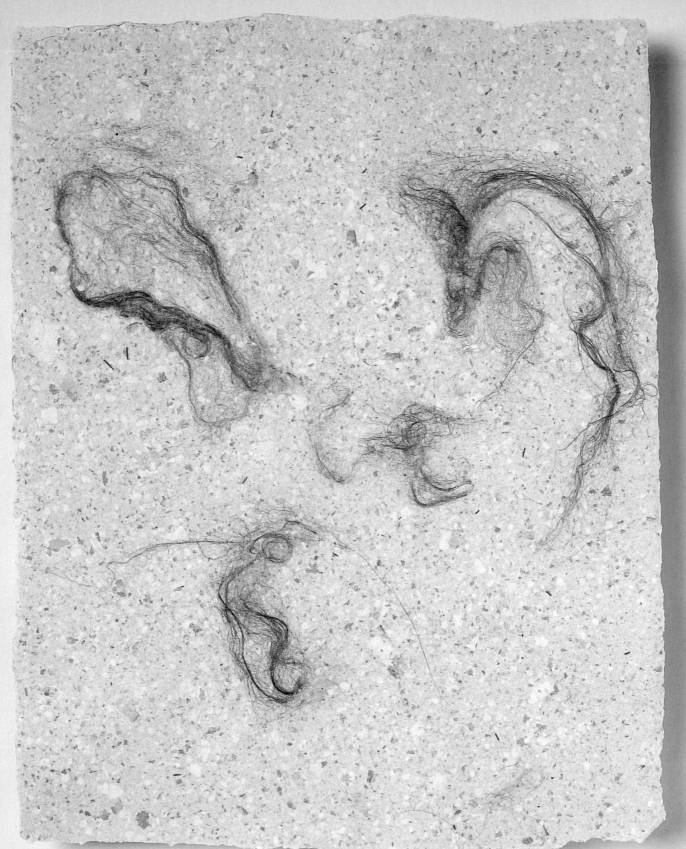

PURE PLANT PULP PAPER

This recipe does NOT include recycled paper pulp and makes beautiful strong dark green sheets. Cooking breaks down the leaf fibers considerably. One large paper grocery bag full of ivy was gathered for this recipe. After removing the thick stems and cooking the leaves, I had approximately 5 cups of pure leaf pulp.

▶ **TIP –** Rinsing of the cooked leaves takes time – allow about one hour to get the rinse water clear.

▶ RECIPE

INGREDIENTS

1 large paper grocery bag
    ivy leaves
2 oz. soda ash *or* 4 oz.
    fireplace ash solution
Acid free additive

TOOLS

Large non-reactive pot and
    spoon (stainless steel,
    enamel-coated, or glass)
Large strainer
Hot plate
Blender

INSTRUCTIONS

1. Soak the leaves in water overnight. Rinse them in the strainer.
2. Fill the pot with 4 quarts of water and heat.
3. Before the water boils, add the soda ash or fireplace ash solution and stir until thoroughly dissolved. Bring the water to a boil.
4. Carefully put the leaves in the boiling water.
5. Reduce the heat to a simmer and cook for about 2 hours, stirring every 30 minutes.
6. Drain and rinse the leaves several times until the water runs clear to completely remove the alkaline solution.
7. Add the leaves and acid free additive to the blender container. Follow the additive manufacturer's instructions regarding how much to use. Add water until the blender container is three-quarters full.
8. Blend for 5 seconds.
9. Pour the pulp into the mold. Use your fingers to evenly distribute the pulp.
10. Follow the steps in The Paper Making Process section to make your paper.

CUMIN & MARIGOLD PAPER

Mixing various materials together makes for interesting papers. In this recipe, the colors of cumin powder and dried marigold petals lend gorgeous golden tones to paper. Enlist your creativity by combining textures and colors.

▶ RECIPE

INGREDIENTS

10 dried orange and yellow marigold petals

1 teaspoon ground cumin

1 cup prepared and strained recycled paper pulp

Spray fixative

Sizing *or* acid free additive

INSTRUCTIONS

1. To retain the petals' colors and avoid bleeding, spray them with fixative and let dry *or* blanch them for 5 minutes and allow to cool completely.

2. Add the pulp and sizing or acid free additive to the blender container. Follow the package instructions regarding how much additive to use. Add water to the container until it is three-quarters full.

3. Blend for 30 seconds.

4. Pour the pulp into the mold. Sprinkle the cumin over the pulp.

5. Scatter the marigold petals over the pulp in the mold and stir very gently with your fingers.

6. Follow the steps in The Paper Making Process section to make your paper.

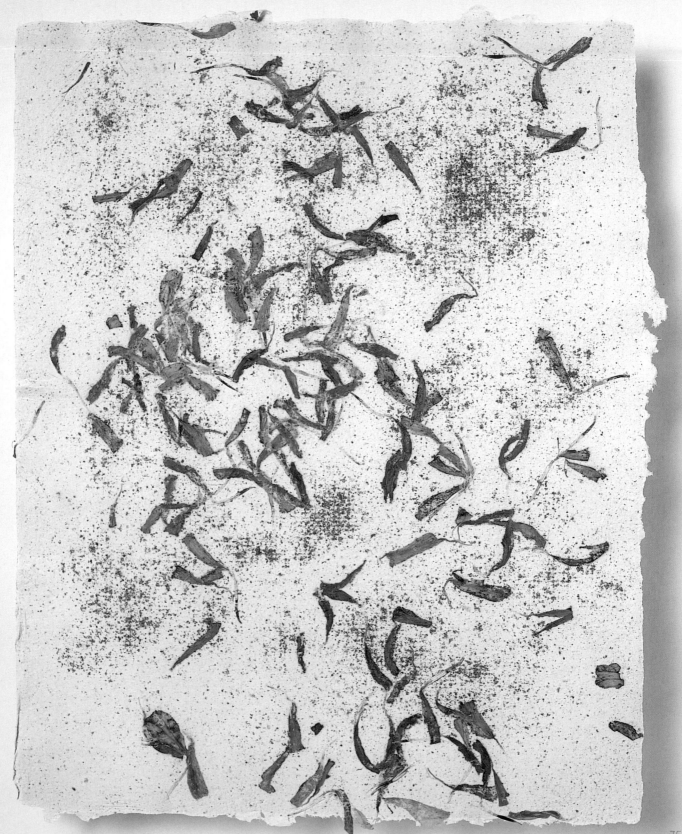

CHILI PEPPER PAPER

For this recipe the chili peppers are crushed in the blender with the paper pulp. The small flat seeds will be visible in the finished sheets and the peppers will fade into the pulp. You could also use just the chili pepper seeds that are sold in the spice section of most grocery stores.

Caution! –

Wear gloves when working with crushed dried chili peppers–they can burn your skin.

▶ RECIPE

INGREDIENTS

10 dried red chili peppers

1 cup prepared and strained recycled paper pulp

Acid free additive

TOOLS

Blender

Whisk

Gloves

INSTRUCTIONS

1. Add the pulp and acid free additive to the blender container. Follow the package instructions regarding how much additive to use. Add water to the container until it is three-quarters full.

2. Blend for 30 seconds.

3. Add the peppers to the blender and pulse for 2 to 3 seconds

4. Pour the pulp into the mold and stir with a whisk to be sure the peppers are evenly distributed.

5. Follow the steps in The Paper Making Process section to make your paper.

Layered Chili Paper

Herbs, flower blooms, and sprigs add texture to papers and look nice when laminated or layered between two couched sheets. Here sprigs of herbs were layered with the chili pepper paper.

Here's how:

1. Make a sheet of chili pepper paper following the previous instructions and couch it.

2. Arrange the herbs or sprigs on top.

3. Make another sheet of chili pepper paper. Couch it on top of the first sheet with the sprigs between.

4. Use your fingers to carefully remove part of the top layer of paper to expose the buds.

5. Press and dry the laminated sheets.

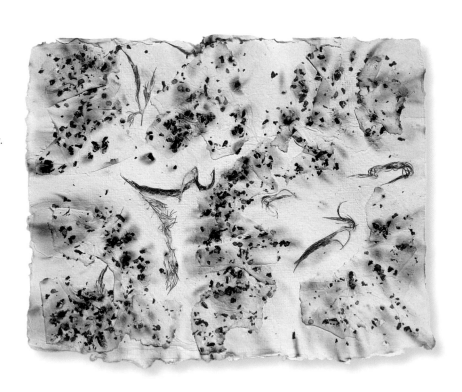

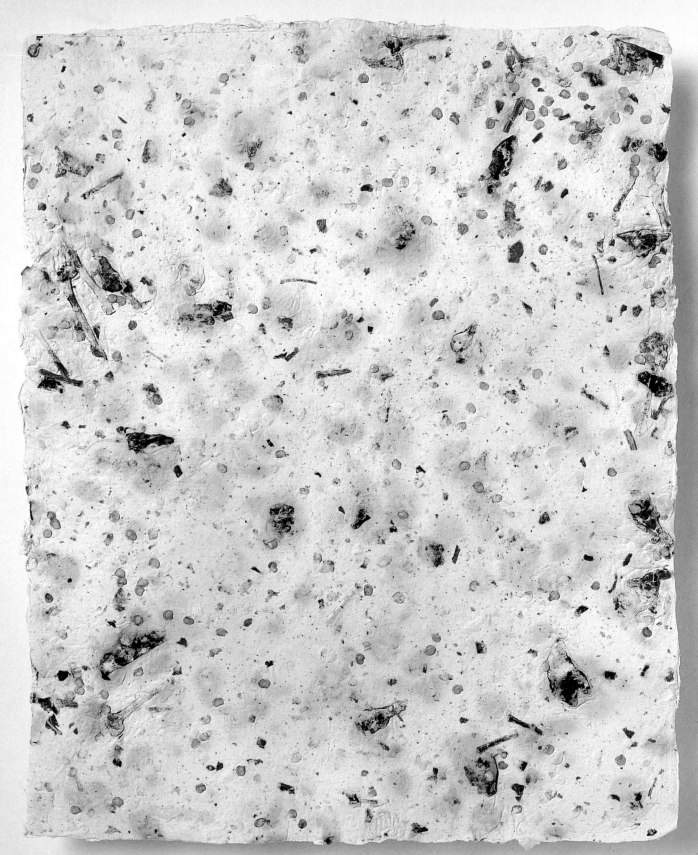

LETTUCE PAPER

The fibers of lettuce leaves give papers personality, texture, and interest, and the natural plant pigments from lettuce leaves can produce very subtle shades in papers. When boiled, the plant materials create a concentrated liquid that can be used to stain (add color to) the pulp. Purchased cotton pulp will take the stain much better than recycled pulps. For a deeper tint, allow the liquid pulp to sit for 4 to 6 hours or overnight before using it to make paper sheets.

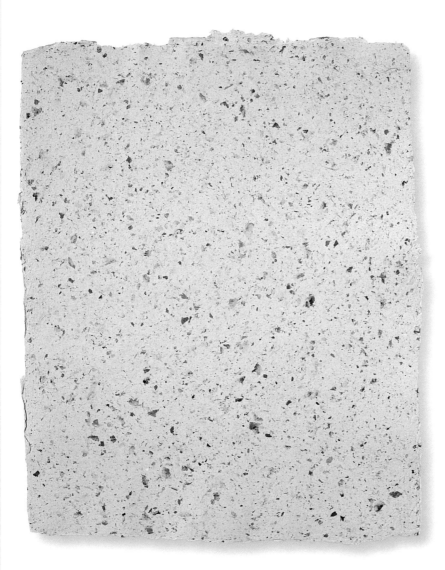

▶ RECIPE

INGREDIENTS

1 cup chopped lettuce leaves

1 cup prepared and strained paper pulp

Acid free additive

TOOLS

Large non-reactive pot and spoon

Large strainer

Stovetop *or* hot plate

INSTRUCTIONS

1. Put the lettuce leaf pieces in the pot and fill it with enough water to cover the plant materials. Bring to a boil.

2. Reduce the heat to a simmer and continue cooking for 1 hour, stirring after 30 minutes.

3. Drain and rinse the leaves, reserving the cooked liquid.

4. Add the paper pulp and acid free additive to the blender. (Follow the package instructions regarding how much additive to use.) Add the reserved liquid to the blender until the container is three-quarters full.

5. Blend for 30 seconds.

6. Add the cooked leaves to the blender and pulse for 2 to 3 seconds.

7. Follow the steps in The Paper Making Process section to make your paper.

BIRCH BARK PAPER

Loose bark from river birch trees makes gorgeous naturally textured paper sheets. You can use this recipe to make papers using any kind of thin tree bark. Thin bark will flatten and adhere to the wet sheets much better than thick bark, and thin bark will not add a lot of weight or thickness to the paper.

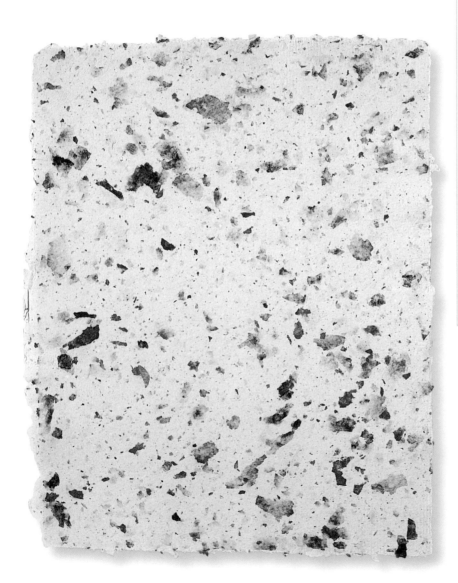

▶ RECIPE

INGREDIENTS

½ cup river birch bark

1 cup prepared and strained recycled
    paper pulp

Acid free additive

INSTRUCTIONS

1. Place the recycled paper pulp in the blender container. Add water until the container is about three-quarters full.
2. Blend for 30 seconds.
3. Put the birch bark in the blender and pulse for 2 to 3 seconds.
4. Follow the steps in The Paper Making Process section to make your paper.

PRESSED DAISY PAPER

Whole pressed flowers are a beautiful addition to paper sheets. Pressed daisies and other pressed flowers generally don't bleed into the paper if they are added to the wet pulp after it's been poured into the mold. For best results, keep the paper pressed flat between two couch sheets until it's completely dry.

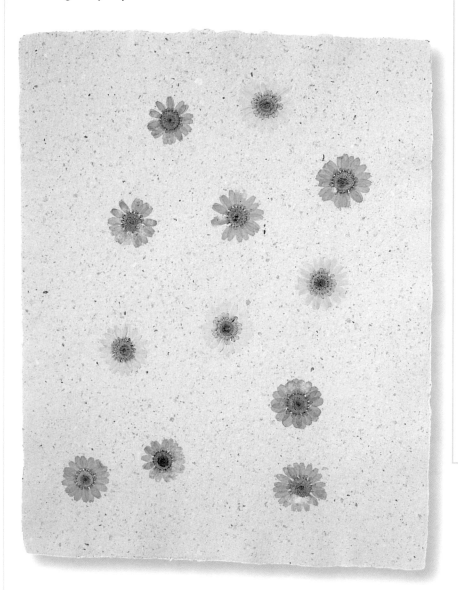

▶ RECIPE

INGREDIENTS

12 pressed white-and-yellow daisies

1 cup prepared and strained recycled paper pulp

INSTRUCTIONS

1. Place the recycled paper pulp in the blender container. Add water until the container is about three-quarters full.

2. Blend for 30 seconds.

3. Pour the pulp into the mold. Carefully place the daisies in the pulp.

4. Gently press the daisies into the wet pulp until they are not floating above the pulp (but try not to completely submerge them), then lift the mold out of the vat.

5. Follow the steps in The Paper Making Process section to make your paper.

DRIED THISTLE PAPER

For this recipe I used the center and outer edges of a large purple dried thistle head. Thistles grow wild along roadsides and in unmowed pastures—you may be able to gather dried thistles late in the summer months. Some parts of thistles are stiff and thick and will not soften in water. Try to use smaller pieces and experiment with them to find the best parts for making flat paper sheets.

▶ RECIPE

INGREDIENTS

½ cup dried thistle pieces

1 cup prepared and strained recycled
   paper pulp

TOOLS

Blender

INSTRUCTIONS

1. Place the recycled paper pulp in the blender container. Add water until the container is about three-quarters full.
2. Blend for 30 seconds.
3. Pour the pulp into the mold
4. Add the thistle pieces to the pulp and stir one time with your fingers.
5. Follow the steps in The Paper Making Process section to make your paper.

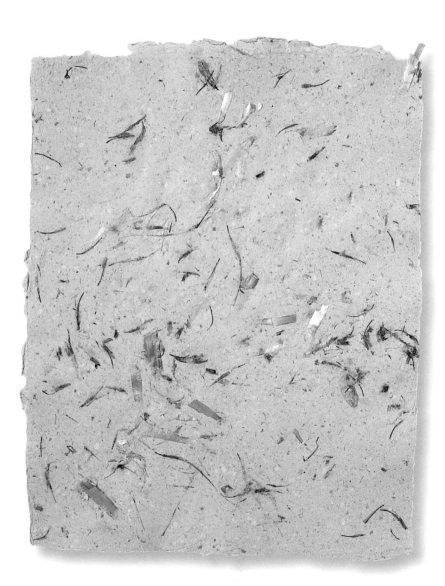

CINNAMON PAPER

Mixing ground cinnamon with crushed cinnamon sticks makes a wonderfully fragrant, textured sheet. You can revive the scent of cinnamon papers with a few drops of cinnamon essential oil.

▶ RECIPE

INGREDIENTS

3 thin cinnamon sticks

1 teaspoon ground cinnamon

1 cup prepared and strained recycled paper pulp

TOOLS

Blender

Small zipper-top plastic bag

Hammer

INSTRUCTIONS

1. Put the cinnamon sticks in the plastic bag. Pound them with a hammer to crush them.

2. Place the recycled paper pulp in the blender container. Add water until the container is about three-quarters full.

3. Blend for 30 seconds.

4. Put the crushed cinnamon pieces in the blender and pulse for 2 to 3 seconds.

5. Pour the pulp into the mold. Sprinkle the ground cinnamon on top of the wet pulp. Gently move the cinnamon pieces and ground cinnamon around until they are evenly distributed.

6. Follow the steps in The Paper Making Process section to make your paper.

7. *Option:* Tie bundles of dried cinnamon sticks or other stems or twigs to the individual sheets with ribbons or twine.

PLANTS TO USE FOR PAPER MAKING

This list includes only a few of the dried and fresh plant materials that can be used to make papers. Almost any leaf or flower can be dried and added to your papers–the only limitations are your imagination and your willingness to learn about and experiment with processing plant fibers.

To retain most of the original qualities and colors of flowers, blooms, and leaves, press them and add them to the wet pulp or to the papers after they are dried. If you're adding fresh leaves to the pulp, they should be cooked to remove any impurities (thicker leaves should be cooked in an alkaline solution) and thoroughly rinsed. Dried materials will retain their color longer and will result in better archival quality papers; manufactured materials like fabric, recycled paper, coffees, and processed textiles will speed the deterioration of your papers. To avoid disappointment, consider how you will be using your papers before you make them.

Flowers
Baby's Breath
Bachelor Buttons
Carnations
Chrysanthemums
Cornflowers
Daffodils
Geraniums
Gladiolus
Hibiscus
Hollyhock
Iris
Larkspur
Lavender
Lilies
Marigolds
Pansy
Phlox
Queen Anne's Lace
Roses
Small Daisies
Statice
Strawflowers
Sunflowers
Wisteria

Leaves
Beech
Birch
Chestnut
Elm
Grapevine
Ivy
Kudzu
Maple
Oak
Willow

Leaves & Flowers
Hosta
Hydrangea
Crepe Myrtle

Grasses, Mosses & Other Greenery
Cedar
Ferns–All Varieties
Juniper
Lawn Grass
Mosses
Ornamental Grasses
Pine Needles
Seaweed Grass

Straw
Wheat

Vegetables & Herbs
Apples
Basil
Beets
Bell Peppers
Carrot Tops and Roots
Chilies
Cinnamon
Cucumbers
Curry
Dill
Lettuce
Mint
Onions
Oranges
Oregano
Paprika
Parsley
Rosemary
Saffron
Thyme
Tomatoes
Tumeric
Zucchini

Chapter

4.

HANDMADE PAPER PROJECTS

I created the projects in this section with the intention of inspiring you to think about using your handmade papers in different ways. Recipes for most of the papers I used, along with photos, are included in the *Paper Making Recipes* section. Here are some general tips for working with handmade papers.

- Play with tearing and layering your papers. Reposition them until you are happy with the results, then glue everything together.
- Almost all papers have a grain or direction in which they can be most easily folded or torn. The best way to determine the grain is to test it by gently attempting to fold it horizontally and vertically. Notice which is easier. That's how the grain runs.
- If you glue papers and other materials with PVA, they can be easily removed with a little water.
- To cover any unsightly spots in a piece of paper, simply layer another piece of paper on top of it or cover it with another leaf or flower petal.
- Sometimes the most beautiful pressed leaf or flower is not the most perfect one. This is also true for handmade papers. The advantage of working with handmade papers and botanicals is the natural art that is created when you allow the fibers to blend together to form one-of-a-kind pieces. The natural imperfections that sometimes appear in your papers can be used to enhance your finished designs.
- Personalize! When making gifts for friends and family members, find out what their favorite flowers and plants are. Use that information to concoct unique, one-of-a-kind gifts.

CUTTING YOUR PAPERS

Cutting with a rotary cutter.

Use scissors, a rotary cutter with decorative blades, or a craft knife to cut your papers. Cut on a self-healing mat to protect your work surface.

Cutting with a craft knife, using a metal ruler as a guide.

Cutting with scissors.

TEARING PAPERS

You can also tear papers. The torn edges will not be perfectly straight; if the paper gets creased or wrinkled, don't worry—it will flatten when you glue it. An additional benefit of tearing is the whiff of wonderful fragrance some papers provide. Mint Paper, for example, releases scent each time you peel back a torn edge, and the scent remains on your fingers for several minutes.

Using a metal deckle edge ruler to quickly tear an uneven edge.

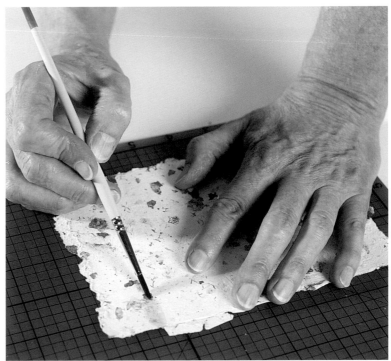

Step 1: To create an almost straight torn edge, first fold the paper where you want to tear it. Use a clean paintbrush to apply water along the fold. (A drop of water can also help separate the fibers if your paper is highly textured.)

Step 2: Hold the paper on either side of the fold with the thumbs and forefingers of both hands and tear toward your body. For best results, tear in small sections—about ½" at a time.

Grass Paper–See Paper Making Recipes *section.*

GRASS PAPER
Greeting Card

Handmade papers make beautiful, personal cards for all occasions. Who would have thought that grass clippings would make such a pretty paper for a greeting card. Here grass paper is paired with pressed weeds to make a naturally beautiful card. Some weeds rival ornamental plants and shrubs in their appeal. However, take care to avoid the poisonous ones. I found these interesting leafy weed stems in my backyard.

Supplies

Ingredients and Tools for Grass Paper
(See the Paper Making Recipes
section.*)*

3 weed stems with leaves

Flower press

Writing paper or card blank, 5" x 7"

Glue

▶ **TIP –** Because it's difficult to write on many handmade papers, I often write my personalized greeting on another sheet of paper and slip it inside the card. Simply cut a sheet of writing paper a little smaller than the handmade paper card, fold it, place inside the card. To hold the paper in place, you can wrap fibers or ribbons around the folded edge, or add small dots of glue along the crease in the card to hold the writing paper in place.

Instructions

Make the Paper:

Make one 7" x 10" piece of Grass Paper, or use a 5" x 7" deckle to make the paper. Use the Grass Paper recipe in the *Paper Making Recipes* section. After pouring the grass paper pulp into the mold, carefully position the weed stems in the pulp inside the mold and lift the mold to make the sheet. When the sheet is couched, dried, and pressed the weeds will adhere to the paper.

Assemble:

1. Fold the paper piece in half so you have a 5" x 7" card.
2. Carefully tear the grass paper to fit on the front side of the 5" x 7" card. Glue it to the card.
3. Slip the writing paper piece inside the card and glue it to the fold of the card with dots of glue.

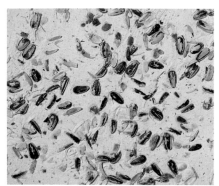

Seed Paper–See Paper Making Recipes *section.*

PLANTABLE SEEDS
Greeting Card

This plantable seed paper contains sunflower seeds. They were mixed with the pulp in the blender. This makes a great gift for a gardener friend. The paper can be planted in the spring just like regular seeds would be planted. Be sure to include the planting instructions inside the card.

Supplies

Ingredients and Tools for Plantable Seed Paper *(See the Paper Making Recipes section.)*

Sunflower seeds with hulls

Writing paper, 8" x 6"

Glue

▶ **TIP –** Make an instructional greeting entitled *Plant These Seeds of Friendship* on a piece of paper and slip it inside the card.

Instructions

Make the Paper

Make one 8½" x 11" piece of Plantable Seed Paper, using the recipe in the Paper Making Recipes section. Add the sunflower seeds to the blender and pulse before pouring the paper into the mold.

Make the Card

1. Tear the plantable seed paper to make a 9" x 6" piece.
2. Fold the piece in half to make a 4½" x 6" card.
3. Fold the writing paper in half to make an insert for the card.
4. On the left inside, write instructions for using the seed paper. On the right inside, write a greeting.
5. Slip the folded paper inside the card and attach to the crease of the card with dots of glue.

Include these instructions or print on the inside of card.

Plant These Seeds of Friendship

Tear off bits of paper containing the seeds and plant them directly in the ground when danger of frost is past. The paper will compost naturally, and the seeds will sprout and grow to be sunflowers.

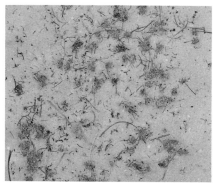

Queen Anne's Lace Paper–See Paper Making Recipes *section.*

QUEEN ANNE'S LACE
Greeting Card

This paper is made with dried Queen Anne's lace in the fibers. The paper has a very slight pink color because a little pink recycled paper was used to make the pulp. Pressed bridal veil flowers and rue stems decorate the front of the card. This card would be a lovely card to accompany a wedding gift.

Supplies

Ingredients and Tools for Queen Anne's Lace Paper *(See the Paper Making Recipes section.)*

1 pressed bridal veil flower

2 pressed rue stems with leaves

Glue

Writing paper, 8" x 6"

▶ TIP – You can enclose your cards in purchased envelopes or use an envelope deckle to make matching or coordinating envelopes for cards when you're making papers. Be sure to assemble the envelope and measure the size before making the card to be sure the card will fit inside.

Instructions

Make the Paper
Make one 8½" x 11" piece of Queen Anne's Lace Paper, using the recipe in the Paper Making Recipes section.

Assemble the Card
1. Tear the Queen Anne's lace paper to make a 9" x 6" piece. Fold the piece in half to make the card.
2. Glue the rue leaves and the bridal veil flower to the front of the card, using the photo as a guide.
3. Fold the writing paper to make an insert for the card. Glue the insert to the inside back of the card. Write your greeting on the insert.

VEGGIE
Candle Cylinders

Vegetable parings make unique and interesting designs on papers. Here, they're paired with tissue paper to make translucent covers for glass candle cylinders. The process for making these colorful vegetable strips is similar to the one used in ancient times for making papyrus, where strips of the fibrous inner pith from stalks of the *Cyperus papyrus* were cut and laid in overlapping layers, then pressed to create sheets.

Supplies

Vegetable material

    Onion skin

    Zucchini

    Red bell pepper

3 glass cylinders

1 sheet cream tissue paper

3 candles

PVA glue

Water

Wax paper *or* plastic wrap

Paper Towels

Photo and paper protectant spray

Spray fixative

TOOLS

Vegetable slicer *or* paring knife

Cutting Board *or* other flat work
    surface

Brayer *or* roller tool

Cook top

Vegetable steamer

Pencil

Ruler

Small plastic container

Paint brush

Instructions

Prepare the Veggies

1. Peel a strip of skin from the top of the onion. Use the slicer or a knife to slice the bell pepper and zucchini lengthwise into strips.
2. Cook the bell pepper and zucchini slices in the vegetable steamer for 2 to 3 minutes. Remove and put them on a flat surface covered with paper towels. Let them cool.
3. Place wax paper or plastic wrap on a cutting board or other flat work surface. Cover with several layers of paper towels. Lay the cooked vegetable strips on top. Completely cover your tool and work surface with wax paper or plastic wrap to avoid stains.
4. Use the brayer or roller tool to press the zucchini and bell pepper slices, removing the soft parts from the skin.
5. Allow the veggie pieces to dry completely.

Assemble

1. Lay the tissue paper on a flat surface. Roll the sides of the glass cylinders across it, marking the edges with the pencil.
2. Place the ruler on top of the marked lines and tear the tissue by pulling it against the edge of the ruler.
3. Mix water with PVA glue in a small plastic container. Using a paint brush, apply the diluted PVA to the torn tissue pieces. Cover the cylinders with the paper pieces, pressing out any air bubbles.
4. Brush diluted PVA to the backs of the onion skin, red pepper slices, and zucchini slices to the cylinders as shown. Allow the glue to dry.
5. Spray the dried cylinders with spray fixative. Let dry.
6. Place the cylinders over the candles.

A Book Maker's Toolbox

Awl, for punching holes

Scissors, for cutting lighter weight papers

Craft knife with extra blades, for cutting thicker papers

Thread (hemp, waxed linen, or any other strong thread or string that will not stretch), for binding

Large-eye needle, for sewing

PVA (polyvinyl acetate) glue. PVA glue is specially formulated to dry fast and is flexible enough to allow adjustments to be made without ruining your covers. It contains less water than craft glue and contains a preservative to prevent mold.

Pencil, for marking

Eraser, for erasing pencil marks

Metal ruler, to use as a guide for cutting or tearing papers, and for measuring

Cutting mat, to protect your work surface and aid in making straight cuts

Bone folder, for creasing

Brayer or roller tool, for smoothing

Metal binder clips in a variety of sizes

Paper press *or* boards and heavy book, bricks, etc., to keep the papers flat while the glue dries.

Wax paper, to keep the covers and pages separated while the glue dries.

Thick cardboard, to cover your work surface when punching holes and cutting pages and covers.

Making Handmade Books
GENERAL INSTRUCTIONS

Handmade papers make beautiful book covers, and handmade books make beautiful gifts. You will need handmade paper for the covers, text paper for the inside of the book, and a few basic tools. Following are general instructions that can be used to make a hardcover book of any size. Making a book is a four-step process. Here are some considerations for each step:

Step One: Choosing the theme
• When making a gift, consider the recipient's favorite things, colors, animals, or fabrics.
• Consider how you will use the book or, if it is to be a gift, how the recipient will use it.

Step Two: Selecting materials
• Use a smooth text weight paper if the book is intended to be a journal. Thicker, textured papers don't work well for writing, but they are wonderful backgrounds for stories about nature and for attaching pressed flowers and leaves, notes, pictures, or postcards.
• For a hardcover book, you will need thick book board or thick poster board (it is stronger than regular cardboard) to use as a base for the cover. Plastic glass, metal, and wood also make good hardcovers.
• When you make your first book cover, practice with some scrap papers. After you understand how the process works, use your precious sheets of handmade papers.

Step Three: Designing the cover and pages
• Play with the materials and have fun with recycling and using new materials.
• You can cut sheets of paper for pages to size and stack them for binding or you can fold large sheets of paper to create pages. Folding a large sheet in half creates a folio (four pages). A quarto (eight pages) is created when you fold a sheet in half twice and trim the folds on one edge. An octavo (sixteen pages on eight paper pieces) is a page folded in half three times–fold twice and trimmed, then folded and trimmed again.

Step Four: Constructing the book
• Be sure that the grain of the paper runs parallel to the spine. Sometimes with handmade paper, the sheets may not have an obvious grain. If you cannot determine the exact grain, then either way should work.
• If you put glue on one side of your paper, it could shrink unevenly as it dries. This can be avoided by putting glue on both sides or you can put it just on the corners–and use a paper press or heavy weights with boards to hold the book covers flat as they dry.

Making a Book, Step by Step
Protect Paper
Because books might get a lot of use and be handled more than other handmade paper projects, I like to spray the handmade paper that I am using for the covers with Photo and Paper Protectant Spray. After making, pressing, and drying the handmade paper, spray the piece with photo and paper protectant. Allow to dry.

Assemble the Text Pages
1. Cut and/or fold your pages to the desired size.
2. Stack the sheets of your chosen paper so they are straight and aligned.
3. Use an awl to punch small holes along the spine edge, 1/8" away from the edge. Thread a needle with hemp or waxed linen thread. Stitch through the holes to join the pages. Tie a knot in the ends of the thread to secure and trim. You can also glue groups of folded pages together along the folds.

Make the Covers

1. Use a craft knife and metal ruler to cut the book board into two pieces to make the front and back covers. Cut the cover boards ½" wider and longer than the text page size.
2. Use your handmade paper to cover the boards for the back and front covers. You will need two pieces of handmade paper. The handmade paper needs to be ½" larger on all sides than the boards for the front and back covers.
3. Place the handmade paper piece for the front cover on the surface, wrong side up. Apply glue to the paper to within ½" of each edge. Position the cover board on the glue-coated paper, pressing it in place so it sticks. Flip it over. Use a brayer or roller tool to roll out any bubbles or creases, working from the center to the edges.
4. Turn over the covered board. Fold and trim the corners to miter them. Use the bone folder to crease the paper at the edges of the board.
5. Apply glue to the edges of the paper. Wrap the paper around the edges of the board, pulling it tight and securing it on the back of the board. Use the brayer or roller tool to smooth the folded edges and corners.
6. Repeat steps 2 through 5 to make the back cover.

Make & Attach the Spine

1. Measure the thickness of the stacked text pages. Measure the thickness of the two covers. This is the *actual spine* width. Add the two measurements plus 1½". This is the width of the spine piece for cutting.
2. Measure the length of the cover. Add 2". This is the length of the spine piece.
3. Use these spine width and spine length measurements to cut two pieces of handmade paper for the spine piece.
4. Place one of the spine pieces on your work surface. Position the covers side by side on top of the spine piece, leaving a gap between them equal to the width of the *actual* spine. Leave equal margins at top and bottom of spine piece. See Fig. 2 for how to position covers on spine piece. Lightly mark the placement of the boards. Remove the boards.
5. Put glue on the side sections of the spine, where you have marked the area for the cover placement. (See Fig. 1.) Reposition the board covers on the spine piece to attach them to the spine. (See Fig. 2)
6. Put glue on the top and the bottom exposed portions of the paper spine piece. (See Fig. 2) Fold the margins to the inside over the top and bottom edges of the boards.
7. Trim 2½" off the length of the remaining spine piece. Apply glue to the wrong side of this piece. Position it to cover the inside of the other spine piece and the edges of the boards. The cover is complete.

Assemble

1. Cut two pieces of handmade or decorative paper to line the insides of the covers. They should be ⅛" smaller on the three sides–top, bottom, and outside than each of the opened covers, with 2" added to the spine sides as flaps. (See Fig. 3) Fold the flaps to the inside. (The flaps will be attached to the first and last pages of the text section.)
2. Glue the lining pieces to the inside of the front and back covers, leaving the flaps loose and lining up the edges of both pieces at the spine. Use the brayer or roller tool to smooth the liner papers and remove any bubbles, rolling from the center to the outer edges.
3. Apply glue to the backside of the flaps. Attach them to the first and last pages of the text section. Press firmly to be sure they are adhered.
4. Place pieces of wax paper between the front and back covers and the first and last pages. Carefully close the book, making sure the first and last pages are securely glued to the liner flaps.
5. Place pieces of wax paper on the outside of the front and back covers. Place the closed book in a paper press for 24 hours. If you do not have a paper press, place the wax-paper-wrapped book on a flat surface, such as a board. Put bricks, heavy books, or other weights on top. Leave in place for 24 hours.

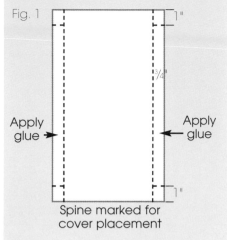

Fig. 1

1"

¾"

1"

Apply glue →

← Apply glue

Spine marked for cover placement

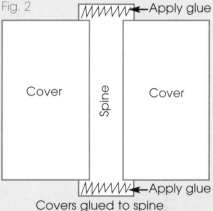

Fig. 2

Apply glue

Cover

Spine

Cover

Apply glue

Covers glued to spine

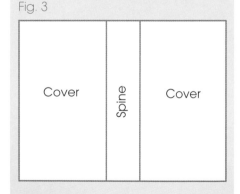

Fig. 3

Cover

Spine

Cover

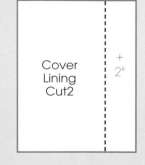

Cover Lining Cut 2

+ 2"

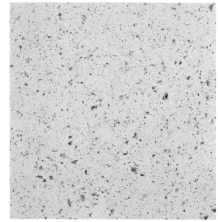

Lettuce Paper–See Paper Making Recipes *section.*

LETTUCE LEAF PAPER
Journal

Lettuce Leaf Paper makes a colorful cover for a journal. It would make a lovely gift for a gardener or a cook. The front and back covers for this book measure 8" x 5½".

Supplies

Text paper, 7½" x 5"–number of pages of your choice

2 cover boards, each 8" x 5½"

2 pieces Lettuce Paper, 8½" x 11"

2 pieces of paper to line the covers (your choice–decorative paper, plain colored paper, or handmade paper), 8½" x 11"

Book making tools (See *A Book Maker's Toolbox* for a list.)

Photo and paper protectant spray (optional)

Instructions

See "Making Handmade Books, General Instructions" for detailed instructions.

Assemble the Pages
Assemble and sew together the number of pages you wish to have for your text pages.

Make the Covers
Use your handmade Lettuce Leaf Paper to cover the cover boards.

Make & Attach the Spine
Make the spine pieces from your handmade Lettuce Leaf paper, following instructions given for *Making Handmade Books.*

Assemble
Assemble as directed.

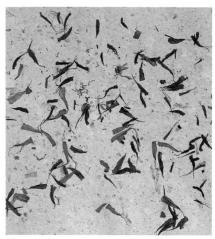

Flower Petal Paper–See Paper Making Recipes *section.*

FLOWER SAVER
Book

I like to make small books and fill the pages with my favorite pressed flowers to give as gifts. The cover of this one is hand-made rose petal and leaves paper; I used pieces of lettuce leaf paper on the inside to hold pressed flowers. You can glue the pressed flowers to the paper with tiny dots of glue. I used red and green yarn fibers to hold the book together. You could substitute several folded pages of text weight paper for the lettuce leaf paper to make a special journal or memory book.

Supplies

1 piece rose petals and leaves paper, 8" x 6" (Use the recipe in the Paper Making Recipes section for Flower Petal Paper and use both dried rose petals and dried rose leaves.)

1 piece Lettuce Paper, 8" x 6" (See the Paper Making Recipes section for instructions.)

Photo and paper protectant spray

Red and green yarn or fibers

Awl

Scissors

Glue

Instructions

1. After making, pressing, and drying the handmade Rose Petals paper, spray the piece with photo and paper protectant. Allow to dry.
2. Fold the rose and leaves paper in half to make the front and back covers.
3. Tear the lettuce leaf paper in half to measure 4" x 6" so they fit inside the folded rose paper cover.
4. Place the lettuce leaf pages inside the folded paper cover.
5. Use the awl to make two holes near the fold through all pieces of paper.
6. Thread the red and green yarn fibers through the holes and tie the ends in a loopy bow near the upper hole.

OTHER IDEAS FOR BINDING BOOKS

There are a lot of different ways to bind your books without making hard covers–just be sure that your materials are strong enough to hold the pages, and that they allow the pages to move easily without tearing.

- Use small strips of paper and glue to make tapes and attach them horizontally across the spine to hold the pages and covers together.
- Use a needle and strong thread or ribbons, raffia, leather laces, or fibers to tie or sew the pages to the covers.
- Make an accordion-style book by folding and gluing or sewing pages together.
- Stack the covers. Place the pages between the covers. Punch or drill holes through the covers and pages. (Copy shops can drill them for you.) Align the holes and hold the pages and covers together with posts and screws or nuts and bolts from the hardware store.
- Thread decorative wires with beads or items that relate to your theme through punched holes in the covers and pages.

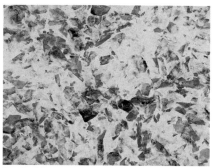

Ivy Leaf Paper–See Paper Making Recipes *section.*

LOVELY LEAVES
Book

This book can be used to store pressed leaves from vacations or special occasions, or as a gift for someone who is moving. We recently moved, and my book holds pressed leaves from my favorite in the backyard of our previous home.

Supplies

1 sheet Ivy Leaf Paper, 8½"x 11"

5 Sheets of absorbent paper for inside 8½" x 11"

Twig

3 pressed leaves–begonia leaves used

Photo and paper protectant spray

Awl

Raffia

Scissors

Glue

Instructions

1. After making, pressing, and drying the Ivy Leaf Paper, spray the piece with photo and paper protectant. Allow to dry.
2. Fold the ivy leaf paper in half to create the front and back covers for the book.
3. Assemble the absorbent papers for the inside of the book. Fold the sheets in half to measure 8½" x 5½" to fit inside the folded ivy leaf paper cover.
4. Use the awl to make two holes near the folded spine through all three pieces of paper.
5. Thread a piece of raffia through each set of the holes. Place the twig near the fold on the front cover and secure it by tightly tying the raffia in bows around the twig. Trim the ends of the raffia.
6. Glue the pressed begonia leaves to the front cover.
7. Your pressed memories can be glued onto the inside pages of the book.

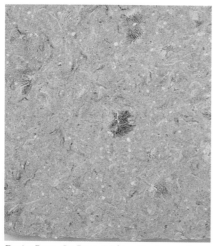

Denim Paper–See Paper Making Recipes *section.*

PAPERMAKERS' RECIPES
Envelopes

The creative process of paper making is so engrossing that it's easy to lose track of how you made your most beautiful sheets. These recipe envelopes provide a way to store paper samples and recipes. I used recycled envelopes from junk mail as a base–they are big enough to hold my notes and strong enough to support the samples. Recycle that junk mail!

Supplies

4 sample pieces of handmade paper, each 4" square (The samples include Denim Paper, Rose Petal and Leaves Paper, Soy Fibers Paper, and Coffee Paper.)

4 recycled envelopes

Glue

Paper making recipes written on pieces of paper that is the width of the envelope plus 1" taller than the envelope

Instructions

1. Cut off the flaps of the envelopes.
2. Cut or tear your handmade pieces of paper to the size of the envelopes.
3. Glue the paper samples to the fronts of the envelopes.
4. Insert the paper recipes in the corresponding envelope with the name of the paper visible above the envelope opening.

Make a Recipe Envelope Book

To make a recipe envelope book, punch holes in the left side of each envelope. Stack them together, aligning the holes, and thread some fibers or ribbons through the holes. Tie the ends together loosely so you can easily add more recipe envelopes later.

Denim PAPER

ROSE PETALS

SOY PAPER

Coffee Paper

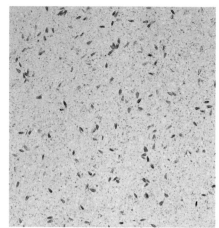

Lavender Paper–See Paper Making Recipes *section.*

BOOK LOVERS
Botanical Bookmarks

Dried lavender buds, oregano, and fresh rosemary make gorgeous bookmarks. These bookmarks will retain some of their herbal scent for a time. When the scents fade, refresh them with a few drops of essential oil.

Bookmarks can be easily made from scraps of paper left over from other projects. You'll find instructions in the Paper Making Recipes section for making Lavender Paper and Herb Paper. Use the Herb Paper recipe to make the oregano paper (using both buds and stems) and rosemary paper.

Supplies

For each bookmark:

1 piece of handmade paper, at least 7" x 3"

Fibers, yarn, or twine in coordinating colors

Hole punch

▶ **TIP –** Bookmarks are a wonderful gift for your bookclub friends. Find out their birthday months and make with papers using the flowers for that month.

▶ **TIP –** As an option, instead of adding the dried flower petals to the paper pulp, glue pressed flowers onto the bookmark that is made from a colorful piece of plain handmade paper.

Instructions

1. Carefully tear the handmade paper to make an irregular rectangular shape approximately 6" long and 2" wide.
2. Use a hole punch to make a hole in one end of the bookmark.
3. Thread fibers or twine through the hole and loop using a lark's head knot. (I used green and gold fibers with the rosemary paper, twine with the lavender paper, and violet and green fibers with the oregano paper.)

Pictured at right, left to right: Oregano Bookmark, Lavender Bookmark, Rosemary Bookmark.

PANSY

Thoughts

I send thee pansies while the ye
Yellow as sunshine, purple as
Flowers of remembrance, ever
By all the chiefest of the son
And if in recollection lives r
For wasted days, and dreams that
I tell thee that the pansy "freake
Is still the heart's-ease that the p
Take all the sweetness of a gift
And for the pansies send me bac

SARAH DOUDNEY

—74—

saying the French
t, and people used
st and dearest to
ts we grow in our
rian times from
ribed as Love-in-
ng face was said
Titania falling in
Dream.
e with children
affectionate
and-hood and
Herb Trinity,
e one flower,
e best known
for it was
you, you

107

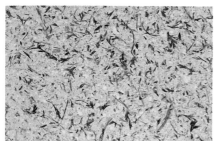

Carrot Top Paper–See Paper Making Recipes section.

TAG ART
Botanical Tags

I used pieces of Carrot Top Paper, Mint Paper, and Birch Bark Paper to make these tags. Instructions for making these papers can be found in the Paper Making Recipes section.

Basic Supplies

For one tag

1 piece of handmade paper, at least 6" x 4"

Raffia, ribbons, or fibers

Embellishments–Pressed leaves or flowers, vellum with computer-generated printing

Hole punch

Glue

▶ TIP – Leftover scraps of your handmade papers can be used to make personalized tags for signs, labels, or gifts. They are easy to make and require only small pieces of paper. Scraps of ribbon, raffia, or fibers can attach them.

▶ TIP – Tearing the edges of the paper adds interest. You can also use decorative edge scissors for cutting the pieces to size.

Instructions

1. Tear the paper into an irregular rectangle approximately 5½" long and 3" wide.
2. Use the hole punch to make a hole (or holes) in the tops of the tags.
3. Thread fibers, raffia, or ribbons through the hole(s).

Door Tag

Mint Paper was used to make this door sign. Make two holes in the top of the tag. Thread lilac and green ribbons through the two holes and knot on the front of the tag. Tie an over-hand knot with the ribbons as shown. Use a computer to print the message on a piece of patterned vellum. Trim and glue to the tag.

Organizer Box Tag

Carrot Top Paper was used here. Make one hole in the center top of the tag. Thread the raffia through the hole. Use a computer to print a label for the contents of the box on a piece of patterned vellum. Trim and glue to the tag. Tie the raffia to the ribbon on the box.

Gift Tag

Birch Bark Paper was used to make this natural gift tag. Punch a hole in the center of the tag. Thread the brown fibers through the hole. Glue a pressed leaf or flower to decorate the tag. Use the fibers to tie the tag to a gift.

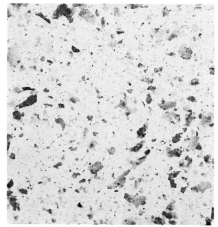

Birch Bark Paper–See Paper Making Recipes section.

BARK & HERBAL
Decorative Accessories

A paper cone and paper-covered balls are just the right style for a rustic décor. Plastic foam shapes are very easy to cover with handmade papers, and they make great tabletop decorations and seasonal ornaments. The cone, which is wrapped in Birch Bark Paper, has a wire hanger and cedar, eucalyptus, and laurel leaves inserted in the top. The balls are covered with Herb Paper made with rosemary leaves.

Supplies

1 piece Birch Bark Paper, 8½" x 11"

1 piece Rosemary Paper, 8½" x 5"

Plastic foam shapes—6" cone, 4" ball, 2½" ball

5 stems dried brown eucalyptus

3 stems dried brown cedar

3 stems dried brown laurel leaves

Glue

Brown-wrapped wire

Wire cutters *or* stem cutters

Optional: Low temp glue gun and glue sticks

▶ TIP – You could use the same techniques to make colorful holiday ornaments, substituting Flower Petal Paper made with red roses and Mint Paper. Add pressed roses, leaves, and a ribbon hanger.

Instructions

Make the Papers
Use the instructions in the Paper Making Recipes section to make Herb Paper with rosemary leaves and Birch Bark Paper.

Make the Cone
1. Wrap the Birch Bark Paper around the cone, letting the paper extend above the wide end. Glue to secure.
2. Trim the cedar and laurel stems to between 4" and 6". Insert them at the back of the wide end of the cone.
3. Trim the eucalyptus stems to between 3" and 5". Insert them at the front and sides of the wide end of the cone.
4. Cut a 24" piece of brown-wrapped wire. Coil the wire to create a hanger shape. Insert the ends into the sides of the cone.
Option: Use hot glue to secure the stems and wire hanger.

Cover the Balls
1. Tear the rosemary paper into 2" pieces.
2. Glue the pieces, overlapping them, to cover the balls.

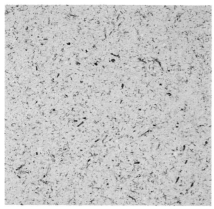

Moss Paper–See Paper Making Recipes *section.*

PRESSED BOTANICALS
Framed Art

The natural shapes of pressed leaves and ferns can be embedded in handmade papers to make beautiful works of art for your walls. These framed pieces can work with any style of room or picture frame. The barn wood frames have a casual, rustic look, but simply changing the frame could make the pieces suitable for traditional, contemporary, or formal rooms.

Supplies

Ingredients for making 2 sheets of Moss Paper

1 pressed fall leaf

4 pressed fern fronds

2 barn wood frames with glass

Photo and paper protectant spray

Scissors

Pencil

Instructions

Make the Paper

1. Using the instructions in the Paper Making Recipes section, prepare enough Moss Paper pulp to make two 8½" x 11" sheets of Moss Paper.
2. After pouring the first sheet of moss pulp into the mold, place the fern fronds on the pulp inside the mold. Push some of them down into the pulp so they almost disappear and lift the mold out of the vat. Remove the sheet from the mold.
3. After pouring the second sheet of moss pulp into the mold, place the fall leaf on the pulp inside the mold and lift the mold out of the vat. Remove the sheet from the mold.
4. After couching, the leaves will be embedded in the paper sheets. Press and dry the sheets.

Assemble

1. Spray the papers with photo and paper protectant and let dry.
2. Remove the backing pieces from the barn wood frames.
3. Place the backing of one frame on the fern paper, positioning the fern in the frame opening. Trace around the backing and trim the paper to fit inside the frame. Place the paper in the frame. Replace the frame back.
4. Place the backing from the second frame on the leaf paper, positioning the leaf in the frame opening. Trace around the backing and trim the paper to fit inside the frame. Place the paper in the frame. Replace the frame back.

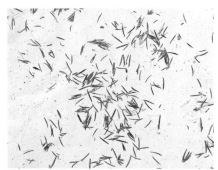

Juniper Paper–See Paper Making Recipes *section.*

Supplies

Ingredients for making paper

¼ cup brown eucalyptus leaves

1 pressed maple leaf

1 floating glass frame

Scissors

Pencil

Instructions

Make the Paper:

Use the instructions for Juniper Paper in the Paper Making Recipes section to make a sheet of paper. Add brown eucalyptus leaves to ¼ cup of cedar stems and the paper pulp in the blender container before pulsing.

Assemble:

1. Remove the two glass pieces from the floating glass frame.
2. Tear an uneven piece of the eucalyptus and cedar paper a little smaller than the glass area of the frame.
3. Position the pressed leaf on the paper piece. Put the paper and leaf between the two pieces of glass and replace the glass in the frame.

FLOATING LEAF
Framed Art

A sheet of handmade paper with irregular, torn edges makes a wonderful display in a floating glass frame. This paper, made with eucalyptus leaves and cedar, complements the autumn colors of a pressed maple leaf.

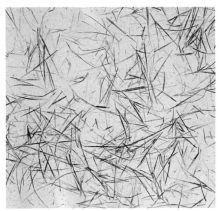

Grass Paper–See Paper Making Recipes *section.*

GRASS PAPER
Lampshade

Handmade papers can make interesting textured covers for lampshades, and they look beautiful with light shining through them. You could make a coordinated set of shades for a chandelier, or do as I did here–use a long-stem martini or a water glass to support a covered shade and put a votive candle in the glass. You'll have a quick, easy centerpiece for a small tabletop.

Supplies

1 sheet of Grass Paper, 8½" x 11"

Chandelier lampshade, 5" tall, 6" diameter

Long-stem martini glass *or* water glass, 10" tall, 4" wide

Votive candle

Glue

Instructions

1. Place the lampshade on its side and roll it across the sheet of grass paper, using a pencil to mark the top and bottom edges.
2. Using scissors, cut out the traced shape.
3. Wrap the cutout paper piece around the lampshade, overlapping the ends of the paper. Holding the paper shape, remove the paper from the lampshade. Glue the edges of the paper shade to secure them. Allow to dry.
4. Put the candle in the glass. Place the paper cover over the shade, and put the shade on the glass.

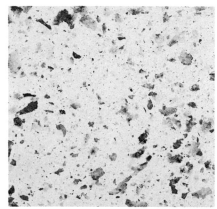

Birch Bark Paper—See Paper Making Recipes *section.*

BIRCH BARK PAPER
Desk Accessories

To make the paper that covers this desk blotter and pencil cup project, I recycled some brown and orange papers to make the pulp, which looked dark brown in the blender. Birch bark and cedar needles were blended with the pulp to make these beautiful nature-inspired sheets. When dry, the sheets were several shades lighter than the wet pulp had been.

Supplies

1 cup birch bark and other ingredients for 4 sheets Birch Bark Paper, 8½" x 11"

1 cup cedar needles

2 cork squares, 12"

Brown corrugated cardboard, 12" x 20"

Antiquing spray

Recycled soup can

Scissors

Ruler

Pencil

Glue

Instructions

Make the Paper

Following the instructions for Birch Bark Paper in the Paper Making Recipes section, mix and measure two separate batches of Birch Bark & Cedar Paper to make four sheets in all. Use ½ cup birch bark and ½ cup cedar for each batch.

Assemble

1. Measure, mark, and cut two 12" x 4½" strips of cork from one of the cork squares. Place the two cut pieces on opposite sides of the other cork square. Glue the cork pieces to the corrugated cardboard.
2. Cut two 2¾" squares of cork to make the base for the soup can.
3. Take the cardboard and cork pad, the soup can, and the two small cork squares outside. Spray them with antiquing spray. Allow to dry.
4. Roll the soup can across one of the paper sheets and mark the length of paper needed to wrap around the can. Add ¼" for overlap and mark.
5. Add approximately 1" to the height of the can and mark this measurement on the paper.
6. Tear the marked paper piece. Wrap it around the can and glue the seam.
7. Glue the three remaining paper sheets to the top of the cork and cardboard blotter, overlapping them slightly.
8. Place the can on one cork square. Glue. Position the other cork square under the first as shown in the photo and glue.

<handwritten>
Monday
Call Peyton – lunch Wed.
pick up dry cleaning

Book Club
7pm.
</handwritten>

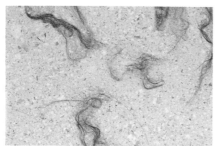

Soy Fibers Paper–See Paper Making Recipes *section.*

SOY FIBERS
Molded Bowl

Soy fibers make strong, durable papers that are especially appropriate for making paper shapes. This bowl is made from two sheets that were couched together for added stability.

Supplies

Ingredients for 2 sheets Soy Fibers Paper, 8½" x 11"

2 plastic bowls with 4" bottoms

Wax paper

Instructions

1. Follow the instructions for making Soy Fibers Paper in the Paper Making Recipes section. Make two sheets.
2. Couch one sheet, then make the second sheet and couch it on top of the first one. Do not dry.
3. Place one plastic bowl upside down on work surface. Position the two couched sheets over the bottom of the bowl, pressing the papers against the bowl and overlapping the sides and edges to shape the papers around the bowl. (Photo 1)
4. Put a piece of wax paper over the wet sheets on the bowl. (Photo 2) Place the other bowl over the wax paper, pushing down on the bowl to press the paper around the bowl that's inside. (Photo 3)
5. Let the paper and bowls dry overnight. The colors will bleed into the paper as it dries.
6. Remove the top plastic bowl and wax paper. Place the plastic bowl bottom down on your work surface, and place the paper bowl inside the plastic bowl. Let the paper bowl sit for several hours until it is completely dry.

How to Mold the Bowl

Photo 1 – *Pressing the paper sheets over the plastic bowl.*

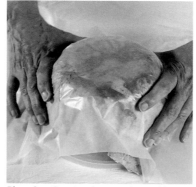

Photo 2 – *Covering the paper sheets with wax paper.*

Photo 3 – *Letting the bowl dry.*

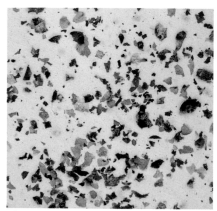

Flower Petal Paper–See Paper Making Recipes *section.*

FLOWER PIN
Paper Jewelry

Flower pins are very easy to create and make perfect gifts for Mother's Day or bridesmaids. This pin was created by my daughter-in-law, JoyAnn Flowers, who makes and sells her own lines of vintage jewelry. She used small pieces of my handmade papers to create this gorgeous design with two flower-shaped templates.

Supplies

5" square of rose and hydrangea
    petals paper

5" square of hosta leaf paper

2 flower-shaped templates, one 3",
    one 2" (Use purchased templates or
    make your own from stiff cardboard
    using the patterns provided.)

1 green shank-type vintage button, ½"

Scissors

Needle and thread

Pin back

Glue

▶ **TIP –** This pin is made with rose and hydrangea petals paper and hosta leaf paper. You'll find instructions for making Ivy Leaf Paper in the Paper Making Recipes section. Use the same recipe to make hosta leaf paper, substituting the hosta leaves for the ivy leaves. To make rose and hydrangea petals paper, use the Flower Petal Paper recipe with rose petals and hydrangea petals.

Instructions

Cut & Fold
1. Make, press, and dry the papers.
2. Use the 3" flower template to trace a shape on the rose and hydrangea petal paper.
3. Use the 2" flower template to trace two small flower shapes on the rose and hydrangea petal paper and two small flower shapes on the hosta leaf paper.
4. Use scissors to cut out the five flower shapes.
5. Fold the four small flower shapes in half. Place them on the large flower shape, overlapping them and alternating the paper types, with the folded edges near the center of the large flower shape. Leave space in the center for the button shank.

Sew & Finish
1. Thread the needle with enough thread to sew through all of the folded flower shapes and the button center. Make small stitches at the center of the folds of each small flower shape near the center of the large flower, stitching through all layers of the folded flowers to the back of the large flower.
2. Sew the button at the center of the large flower.
3. Cut a circle out of rose and hydrangea petals paper to cover the exposed threads on the back of the flower and support the pin back.
4. Place the paper circle on the back of the large flower and position the pin back on top of it. Stitch the pin back to the paper circle and the back of the flower.
5. Glue the edges of the paper circle to the back of the flower.
6. Cut a small piece of rose and hydrangea petals paper to cover the stitched bar of the pin back.
7. Glue the small paper piece to cover the stitched bar.

PATTERNS

Large
flower

Small
flower

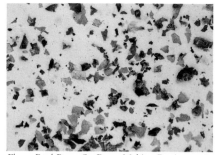

Flower Petal Paper–See Paper Making Recipes *section.*

Supplies

Ingredients for making one sheet of
   Flower Petal Paper, 8½" x 11"

3 dried rosebuds and leaves

Cardboard box *or* papier mache box,
   4" square

Red yarn

Scissors

Glue

Binder clips *or* clothes pins

▶ TIP – After finishing the rose gift box, I noticed the leftover rose petal paper pieces piled on my worktable and thought they resembled a flower. Here they are, repositioned on a card with a dried rosebud center. I formed the scraps of paper into petal shapes and glued them to the front of a greeting card that I made with my handmade paper.

ROSE PETALS
Gift Box

When you give a gift in a box covered with handmade paper, there is no doubt that whatever is inside is special. And a gift in a box like this is really two gifts in one. I covered this little box with air-dried rose paper with embedded rosebuds and embellished it with red fibers and dried leaves and rosebuds.

Instructions

Make the Paper

1. Make one sheet of Flower Petals Paper with dried rose petals and leaves.
2. After removing the wet sheet from the mold place two rosebuds on the paper.
3. Use your fingers to put some wet pulp on top of the rosebuds, covering the stem ends.
4. Couch the wet paper sheet and allow it to air dry.

Cover the Box

1. With the rosebuds centered on the box top, cut a piece of paper to cover the top of the box. Cover the box top, securing it with glue. Hold the paper in place with binder clips or clothes pins until the glue dries.
2. Cover the sides of the box with the remaining paper.
3. Glue the remaining dried rosebud to one side of the embedded rosebuds. Glue three dried leaves to surround the rosebud.
4. Put the gift in the box. Wrap the box with red yarn and tie them in a loose bow on top of the rosebuds.

Rosemary Paper–See Herb Paper in the Paper Making Recipes *section.*

FERN BOTANICAL
Wallhanging

Cork squares, which are easily found at most craft supply or office supply stores, make wonderful frames for showcasing your handmade papers and creating your own wall pieces. This square is covered with torn rosemary paper, a piece of burlap, and a dried fern frond.

Supplies

Ingredients for making one 8½" x 11" sheet of Rosemary Paper

Dark cork square, 12"

Glue

Dried fern frond, 10"

Burlap, 6" x 9"

Wire, 4" (for hanging)

▶ TIP – For a dramatic statement, try hanging a row of four or more on a wall.

Instructions

Make the Paper

Using the instructions for Rosemary Paper found in the Paper Making Recipes section, make a sheet of herb paper.

Assemble the Wall Piece

1. Tear a strip 1" to 1½" wide from each side of the piece of rosemary paper. Set them aside.
2. Turn the cork square as shown in the photo.
3. Glue the burlap horizontally on the cork square.
4. Glue the large piece of rosemary paper on top of the burlap as shown.
5. Position the torn rosemary paper strips around the larger piece of rosemary paper, leaving a small space between the paper pieces. Fold the ends of the strips over the edges of the cork square. Glue the strips to the cork square.
6. Position the fern frond on the rosemary paper and glue in place.
7. Bend the wire to form a hanger loop. Insert the ends of the wire into the back of the top of the cork square.

Tea Paper–See Coffee & Tea Paper in the Paper Making Recipes *section.*

TEA & HERBS
Diary

When I found this small book I thought that it would make a beautiful diary. I added some small scraps of Tea Paper and Oregano Paper, tied it with sheer ribbon, and decorated it with dried nandina stems. The little book was transformed into a beautiful gift.

Supplies

Fabric-covered book, 6½" x 5¼"

Tea Paper, 6" x 4"

Oregano Paper, 5" x 3" (follow the
  Rosemary Paper recipe)

4 dried nandina stems

1⅛ yds. sheer green ribbon, 1" wide

Glue

Ruler

Instructions

1. Tear an uneven piece of the hand-made paper slightly smaller than the book cover.
2. Glue the paper pieces to the book cover, in an overlapping design.
3. Glue the nandina stems to the papers on the front of the book.
4. Wrap the ribbon around the book and tie a bow in the center.

METRIC CONVERSION CHART

Inches to Millimeters and Centimeters

Inches	MM	CM	Inches	MM	CM
1/8	3	.3	2	51	5.1
1/4	6	.6	3	76	7.6
3/8	10	1.0	4	102	10.2
1/2	13	1.3	5	127	12.7
5/8	16	1.6	6	152	15.2
3/4	19	1.9	7	178	17.8
7/8	22	2.2	8	203	20.3
1	25	2.5	9	229	22.9
1 1/4	32	3.2	10	254	25.4
1 1/2	38	3.8	11	279	27.9
1 3/4	44	4.4	12	305	30.5

Yards to Meters

Yards	Meters	Yards	Meters
1/8	.11	3	2.74
1/4	.23	4	3.66
3/8	.34	5	4.57
1/2	.46	6	5.49
5/8	.57	7	6.40
3/4	.69	8	7.32
7/8	.80	9	8.23
1	.91	10	9.14
2	1.83		

INDEX

Continued on next page